LEAD

with

LOVE

LEAD

with

LOVE

10 Heart-Centered Strategies
to Build a More Profitable Business

KAREN SHEPHERD
MSHR, SHRM-CP

O'LEARY
PUBLISHING
The Influencer's Press

ISBN: (print) 978-1-952491-76-4
ISBN: (ebook) 978-1-952491-77-1
Library of Congress Control Number: 2023922068

Developmental Editing by Heather Davis Desrocher
Line Editing by Kat Langenheim
Proofreading by Jennifer Doody
Cover and Interior Design by Jessica Angerstein

Printed in the United States of America

I dedicate this book to my beloved daughter, Lauren Shepherd, not only as my child, but also as a fellow traveler on this remarkable journey of life. As you navigate your own path and continue to grow, learn, and lead, remember that the heartbeat of success lies within you. You are always a shining star!

With a heart full of Gratitude, Love, and Hope,

Mom

LEAD *with* LOVE FOUNDATION

MISSION:

Educate, Connect and Inspire communities, small businesses, and individuals by providing them with the essential training, tools, and resources they need to thrive.

For more information and to make a meaningful charitable contribution, please visit www.leadwithlovefoundation.org. Your support is greatly appreciated!

Lead With Love Tools

Enhance your *Lead with Love* journey
using exclusive, free tools!

Visit www.hrbykaren.com/leadwithlovetools
to access and explore resources to elevate your
leadership experience and thrive!

Contents

Foreword

Jo Ann Blair-Davis, JD

I am privileged to contribute to a book that encapsulates the very essence of effective leadership. Over two decades, I had the distinct pleasure of working closely with the author, during which time we navigated challenges, celebrated victories, and, most importantly, championed a leadership philosophy that has become the cornerstone of our shared success – the *Heart-Centered Approach*. This isn't just a leadership style; it's a way of being, a commitment to forging meaningful connections, and fostering an environment where individuals thrive.

The journey of leading with compassion, empathy, and heart is not a departure from traditional leadership; rather, it's an evolution – a response to the evolving dynamics of the modern workplace and the diverse needs of our teams. It demands a conscious effort, a willingness to learn, and the humility to adapt.

In these pages, you'll find more than strategies; you will discover the lived experiences and lessons learned from a journey marked by authenticity and a genuine commitment to the well-being of individuals and organizations. The 10 Heart-Centered Principles aren't just concepts; they are the result of years of collaboration, resilience, and an unwavering belief in the power of heart-centered leadership. As you immerse yourself in this guide, envision it as an extension of our shared journey as humans.

Beyond the business implications, the *Heart-Centered Approach* is a philosophy that enriches the human experience within organizations. It is a commitment to understanding the intricacies of human dynamics, valuing the unique contributions of each team member, and fostering a culture of trust and collaboration. It is about creating spaces where individuals feel valued, seen, and empowered to contribute their best. It is a promise to build profitable businesses, by investing in people through fulfilling and purpose-driven careers. Embrace the *Heart-Centered Approach,* and witness the profound impact it can have on your leadership, your team, and the success of your business.

To my dear colleague and friend, Karen, thank you for embarking on this journey with me. For years, we lived and breathed the principles written in these pages. This book is a testament to the power of leadership rooted in the *Heart-Centered Approach* and a roadmap for those seeking success in business and fulfillment in their leadership journey. It worked for us for 21 years and can work for your readers, too.

With heartfelt gratitude,
Jo Ann Blair-Davis, JD

Preface

What Powers a Business?

Businesses are driven by profit and productivity but, ultimately, are powered by people. Successful businesses are managed by leaders with compassion, empathy, and heart. In the complicated world of organizations, where policies, procedures, and numbers often take center stage, there also exists a community that goes beyond the conventional practices, and where the *Heart-Centered Approach* dominates the boardroom. It is from this perspective of business that I have written *Lead With Love: 10 Heart-Centered Strategies to Build a More Profitable Business*.

As I embarked on my journey through the maze of human resource management, I became increasingly aware of a fundamental truth: the word human is the first word in Human Resources, and the heart is at the core of every human and organization. Behind each job application, every interview, every training program, and every performance review, there beats a heart – the heart of an individual seeking fulfillment, growth, and purpose within their professional life. It is the collective beating of these hearts that truly defines the culture and success of an organization.

This book is born out of my passion for redefining the way we view individuals, and practice human resources. Leadership is a call to action, an invitation to explore a more compassionate, people-centric approach in the workplace. Through these pages, my goal is to share practical strategies and real-life stories that demonstrate the transformative power of putting the heart at the center of leadership.

Throughout my career, I have had the privilege of witnessing the profound impact a *Heart-Centered Approach* can have on both individuals and organizations. From fostering a sense of belonging to nurturing personal and professional growth, the *Heart-Centered Approach* has the potential to unlock unprecedented levels of employee engagement, satisfaction, and loyalty.

In this book, I hope to inspire business owners, managers, and supervisors to embrace a new perspective – one that recognizes that behind every job title and every payroll entry is a person with dreams, aspirations, and a need for genuine connection. By aligning the goals of individuals with those of the organization, we can create workplaces that not only thrive, but also leave a positive imprint on the lives of those who contribute to them.

The *Heart-Centered Approach* to leadership is a philosophy that can be applied and adapted to organizations of all sizes and industries. I invite you to embark on this journey with me – to explore the transformative potential of infusing heart and humanity into leadership. It is my sincere hope that this book serves as a guiding light on your journey to create a workplace that is not only efficient and productive, but also compassionate and deeply fulfilling – a workplace where hearts flourish, employees thrive, and organizations prosper!

Introduction

The Heart
of Business

*People will forget what you said, people will forget what you did,
but people will never forget how you made them feel.*

— MAYA ANGELOU, POET AND CIVIL RIGHTS ACTIVIST

Maya Angelou's words encapsulates a fundamental truth that lies at the core of the *Heart-Centered Approach*. Well-crafted policies and memos often fade into the background. With a *Heart-Centered Approach*, the focus shifts from dictating rules to engaging in empathetic and open dialogue. It's about creating an environment where employees feel safe expressing themselves, knowing that their voices are heard. The *Heart-Centered Approach* leader recognizes that every conversation is an opportunity to make employees feel seen, valued, and appreciated.

A *Heart-Centered Approach* acknowledges that it's not enough to merely check off tasks and adhere to regulations. Instead, it encourages leaders to infuse their actions with compassion, empathy, and heart. It means going beyond the transactional aspects of business to understand the unique needs and aspirations of each employee. Actions that resonate with the *Heart-Centered Approach* are those that leave a lasting impression – acts of kindness, support during personal challenges, and opportunities for growth and development.

In essence, the *Heart-Centered Approach* leader understands that the impact of actions goes beyond the immediate task at hand and can shape an employee's perception of the organization as a caring and compassionate place to work.

The final part of Angelou's words, *people will never forget how you made them feel,* is the *Heart-Centered Approach.* It highlights the enduring power of emotions, support of its leaders, and the well-being of employees in the workplace. When employees reflect on their experiences within an organization, what lingers is the support they associated with those experiences.

The *Heart-Centered Approach* centers on making employees feel valued, respected, and supported. It's about creating a workplace environment where employees experience a sense of belonging, where their concerns are genuinely heard, and where their well-being is a top priority. Leaders practicing the *Heart-Centered Approach* understand that it's the emotional connection they forge with employees that leaves a lasting imprint.

This emotional connection is not limited to moments of crisis or celebration; it permeates everyday interactions. It's about the warm smile during a routine check-in, the empathetic response to a personal challenge, and the genuine interest in an employee's career aspirations, as well as their interests after 5:00 PM. It's the belief that every employee is more than just a resource; they are an integral part of the organization's journey.

While leaders may have limited time for addressing emotions directly, it's essential to recognize that creating a supportive emotional environment is an investment in the long-term success and sustainability of any organization. When employees feel valued and emotionally supported, they are more likely to be engaged, motivated, and productive, which ultimately contributes to the organization's overall success and bottom line. It's about integrating well-being into the fabric of the workplace culture and leadership practices rather than viewing it as a separate task.

Lead with Love is an exploration of how business owners, supervisors, and managers can embrace this approach to create workplaces where employees not only excel professionally but also feel a profound sense of belonging and well-being. We'll explore the principles, strategies, and real-life examples that demonstrate the transformative power of making employees feel seen, valued, and heard.

THE 10 Principles of the
HEART-CENTERED APPROACH

#1 The Heart-Centered Approach
Lead with compassion, empathy, and heart to optimize human potential.
This provides a more engaged, motivated, and collaborative workforce, which optimizes organizational excellence. It also fosters a workplace culture where individuals feel seen, valued, and supported.

#2 Leadership and Organizational Culture
Take action, influence change, and inspire others to create a sense of purpose and direction.
This provides a positive organizational culture and boosts employee morale.

#3 Employee Well-being
Foster a workplace culture where individuals feel valued, supported, and empowered to navigate the demands of work and life.
This leads to employees who are engaged, productive, and loyal to the organization.

#4 Employee Engagement
Nurture ongoing employee engagement efforts to boost positive outcomes for an organization's success.
This creates enthusiastic contributors who will provide better service and innovative solutions.

#5 Recruitment and Onboarding
Identify individuals who possess the required expertise and soft skills, and who align with the culture. Provide comprehensive orientation, training, and a welcoming environment.
This ensures new employees who are well-prepared and motivated to contribute effectively to the organization's success.

#6 Retention and Turnover

Create a long-term commitment to value individuals for their unique contributions and holistic well-being.

This will minimize turnover and position organizations for successful, long-term employee retention.

#7 Change Management

Embrace change and be willing to evolve and adapt.

This will allow organizations to stay relevant and competitive.

#8 Conflict Resolution

Accept that conflict is unavoidable, and understand it is our actions, reactions, and perspectives that make conflict an opportunity for critical conversation.

This allows leaders opportunities to expand their emotional intelligence, communication skills, empathy, resilience, and personal growth.

#9 Ethics and Values

Guide decision-making, behaviors, and culture to inspire others and ensure the organization operates with integrity and a sense of purpose and fulfillment.

This will foster an environment built on trust, transparency, and accountability for employee morale and productivity, and fortify the organization's reputation and its relationships with stakeholders.

#10 Legal Considerations and Compliance

Uphold the rights of employees and protect the interests of your organization.

This will minimize legal liabilities and damaged reputations and maximize employee morale and workplace harmony.

The Heart-Centered Approach

Lead with compassion, empathy, and heart to optimize human potential.

This provides a more engaged, motivated, and collaborative workforce, which optimizes organizational excellence. It also fosters a workplace culture where individuals feel seen, valued, and supported.

Chapter 1

You Can't Spell HeaRt Without HR

To handle yourself, use your head;
to handle others, use your heart.

—ELEANOR ROOSEVELT

In the dynamic world of Human Resources, where the heartbeat of an organization's success resides, there are three essential qualities: compassion, empathy, and heart. These qualities form the foundation of a progressive and thriving workplace. While they might appear intertwined, each holds its distinct role in forging a path toward not just success, but also the well-being of an organization and its people. To understand the difference between these qualities is to unlock the keys to exceptional leadership.

Compassion

Compassion is the driving force for understanding and alleviating the suffering of others. It means recognizing the trials and tribulations employees face, whether personally or professionally, and genuinely caring about their well-being. A compassionate leader is one who listens without judgment, offers support in challenging times, and champions the cause of the employees. It's a powerful trait that promotes trust and solidarity within the workplace. Employees are more likely to engage, collaborate, and stay committed to an organization where compassion is evident. A compassionate leader can turn workplace challenges into opportunities for growth and connection, fostering a sense of belonging and purpose.

Empathy

Empathy is the ability to step into another person's shoes, to see the world from their perspective, and to understand their emotions and feelings. Empathy is the cornerstone of effective communication and problem-solving. An empathetic leader actively listens to employees, acknowledging their concerns and emotions. This skill fosters better relationships, as employees feel heard and valued. Empathy can be a powerful tool in conflict resolution, as it allows leaders to grasp the root causes of issues and work toward solutions that consider the needs and feelings of all parties involved. An empathetic leader creates an environment where employees are encouraged to express themselves, and where problems are addressed with understanding and fairness.

Heart

Leading with heart involves a genuine commitment to the organization's mission, vision, and values, as well as a sincere desire to see employees flourish. It's the fusion of passion, dedication, and a strong moral compass. A leader with heart goes beyond fulfilling their job responsibilities; they invest themselves emotionally and personally in their role. Such leaders inspire a sense of purpose and motivation among employees as they witness the authentic dedication of their leadership. A leader with heart is a catalyst for fostering a positive workplace culture characterized by trust, integrity, and a shared sense of purpose.

Synergies and Success

Leading with compassion, empathy, and heart is the magic of the *Heart-Centered Approach*. Compassion lays the foundation for understanding the struggles of employees, while empathy sharpens the focus on their emotional needs. Heart brings the passion and dedication to act on this understanding. Together, they create a nurturing and supportive environment where employees not only feel seen, valued, and heard, but are also empowered to reach their full potential.

The *Heart-Centered Approach* is a commitment by leaders to develop human connections within the organization by prioritizing compassion, empathy, and heart. This provides a more engaged, motivated, and collaborative workforce, which thereby optimizes human potential. Optimizing human potential involves unlocking and maximizing an individual's unique signature strengths to contribute effectively to an organization while achieving personal and professional growth, fulfillment, and success. When we look at optimizing human potential, there are five key elements:

1

Leadership: A heart-centered leader interacts with compassion, empathy, and heart, creating authentic connections and an environment where employees feel valued and supported, leading to higher engagement and productivity.

2

Energy: Positive energy in the workplace is contagious. When leaders and employees radiate enthusiasm, passion, and positivity, it energizes the entire organization. This positive energy fuels creativity, innovation, and a willingness to go the extra mile.

3

Interaction: When individuals interact authentically, they build trust and rapport, fostering a sense of belonging and psychological safety. This creates an environment where employees are more likely to express themselves, collaborate, and contribute their unique talents.

4

Collaboration: When individuals collaborate, they tap into diverse perspectives and work collectively towards shared goals. Collaborating from the heart encourages a sense of unity, mutual respect and support, which enhances the creativity and problem-solving capabilities of teams.

5

Empathy: When leaders and team members practice empathy, they create a supportive and inclusive workplace culture. Employees feel valued, heard, and understood, which leads to higher job satisfaction and engagement, and optimizes potential.

Incorporating these elements into business practices recognizes the emotional and psychological well-being of employees, which emphasizes the power of authentic human connections to optimize human potential. Acknowledging the well-being of employees is not just a set of practices, but a mindset that must infuse every leader's decisions and actions.

As Eleanor Roosevelt said, for ourselves, we need to use our heads, and for others, we need to use our hearts. This is the importance of balancing the rational and emotional aspects of leadership. Leaders need to use their *head* to make informed decisions and establish policies, but they should also use their *heart* to relate to and connect with employees on a personal level. The synergy between these two approaches is what drives leadership success, and ultimately leads to the betterment of both employees and the organization as a whole.

> *People don't care how much you know*
> *until they know how much you care.*
> —THEODORE ROOSEVELT

Origins of the Heart-Centered Approach

The *Heart-Centered Approach* is not a new strategy. My first job out of college was in 1987, and I was fortunate to meet my first boss, Morton "Morty" Bobowick, a top-rated attorney at Eastman & Smith Ltd. in Toledo, Ohio. His practice focused on estate planning, estate administration, and tax law. During my interview with Mr. Bobowick, he told me I had a caring heart, a warm smile, and a fun personality, and said I would have a great career in estate planning because of those soft skills. And he was right. For 25 years, that is exactly what I did. I only had the privilege of working with Mr. Bobowick for a year before realizing Ohio was getting too cold and my toes belonged in the sand in Florida. But I will never forget the lessons I learned, and how valued Mr. Bobowick always made me feel.

After living in Florida for four years working for various law firms, I followed my heart to Virginia Beach, VA. In 1992, I started to work with Jo Ann Blair-Davis, who was an attorney at Clark & Stant (now Williams Mullen) there in Virginia Beach. Her practice also focused on the areas of estate planning, estate administration, and tax law.

Jo Ann and Mr. Bobowick had a lot in common. They were both exceptionally smart with extensive tax backgrounds. Both were analytical but compassionate, caring and patient mentors, appreciated fun around the office, and were always top-rated among their peers. Each Thanksgiving I enjoyed spoiling them – with my mother's help – with her perfectly baked "turkey cookies" (sugar cookies shaped like a turkey with a chocolate chip eye, and sprinkled with the perfect amount of cinnamon), and her sponge cakes at Passover. Mr. Bobowick always got his own, even after I moved to Florida!

Jo Ann and I worked together for 21 years, which you do not see very often. How? Because we aligned in leading with the *Heart-Centered Approach*. I never thought of Jo Ann as a boss. Instead, I respected and valued her as a leader who showed me the path of the do's and the don'ts. The main difference between a *boss* and a *leader* is simple: a boss manages employees; a leader inspires and helps employees reach their true potential. And that she did. Jo Ann accepted me for who I was without judgment, and allowed me to be me.

After 21 years together, Jo Ann cut back her hours and shared that I needed to work with a second attorney in the firm. I did not want to do this and told her that I wanted to be the Law Firm Administrator. But Jo Ann told me that I did not have the credentials for that position. As a result, after work I marched myself across the street to Strayer University and asked the advisor what credentials were needed to be a Law Firm Administrator. She shared that I needed a Master's Degree in Human Resources Management, which was a two-year program. Because the firm could not adjust my work schedule to accommodate my school schedule, and my program was not in the legal industry, I lost my job of 21 years.

Thirty years after receiving my Bachelor's Degree, I found myself in uncharted territory. My daughter, Lauren, was in middle school at the time, and I was gone some days for 15 hours. So my 80-year-old mother agreed to move from what she knew, and away from all of her darlings (her children and her grandchildren and great-grandchildren) in Ohio, to help me in Virginia Beach. I am forever grateful for that. I graduated in one and a half years, nearly doubled my GPA from 30 years earlier with a 4.0, and was the proud recipient of the Outstanding Graduate Award. Finally, at 45 years old, I found my purpose – to focus on being *HUMAN* and a *resource,* and continue the legacy of Mr. Bobowick and Jo Ann in leading with the *Heart-Centered Approach.*

I had known since I was 15 years old that there had to be a larger purpose for my life – even though it took me 30 years to find it. When I was 15 years old, my dearest friend, Mindy Prizant, perished in an electrical house fire, which is where I would have been if my mom had allowed me to spend the night after our high school football game. One word – NO – is the reason I lived and now have the opportunity to write this book and inspire you to lead with the *Heart-Centered Approach.*

The word *no* is often seen as a roadblock or a negative response; but it can be a powerful catalyst for personal and professional growth. When viewed as an opportunity, no is about adopting a growth mindset, resilience, and a proactive attitude. **Do not allow someone else's reaction to change the way you move forward.** The Top 10 reasons I love the word *no:*

1. Resilience and Adaptability: No is a chance to build resilience and adaptability. Instead of seeing it as a rejection, see it as an opportunity to learn from the experience. It's an opportunity to bounce back stronger, wiser, and more determined.

2. Creative Problem-Solving: *No* often requires you to think outside the box. It pushes you to come up with creative solutions or alternatives. In business, this can lead to innovative products, services, or processes that you might not have considered if the initial answer had been a *yes.*

3. Feedback and Improvement: *No* can be a source of valuable feedback. It gives you insights into areas where you can improve. It's an opportunity to refine your skills, products, or ideas based on constructive criticism.

4. New Pathways: Sometimes, a *no* redirects you to new and unexplored pathways. You might discover opportunities you hadn't considered before. This redirection can lead to exciting and unexpected adventures – an important thought if you are terminated!

5. Persistence and Determination: *No* can be the driving force behind your determination. It tests your commitment to your goals. Many success stories involve individuals who faced numerous rejections but persisted until they achieved their objectives.

6. Networking and Relationships: Even with a *no* there's the opportunity to establish connections. Reaching out to people who have rejected you can lead to conversations, networking opportunities, and relationships that may benefit you in the future.

7. Empowerment: *No* can be empowering. It reminds you that you have the capacity to take control of your life and career. It's a reminder that you can shape your own destiny and are not obligated to the whims of others.

8. Learning and Growth: Every *no* is a lesson waiting to be learned. It's an opportunity for personal and professional growth – providing the ability to learn from failures. Embracing rejection allows you to continuously evolve and become a better version of yourself.

9. Motivation: *No* serves as a powerful motivator; it can spark resilience and determination. When faced with rejection or obstacles, it can fuel a desire to prove oneself, find alternative solutions, and ultimately achieve success despite initial setbacks.

10. **Character Building:** Facing challenges helps build character – fostering your values, integrity, and moral strength. It is an opportunity to showcase your grace and professionalism in the face of disappointment.

I will always be grateful for my mom's *no*, and have embraced this powerful little word. In the leadership world, where negotiations, decisions, and rejections are a part of the daily routine, understanding how to turn *no* into an opportunity is crucial. By embracing rejection as a stepping stone rather than a dead end, leaders can navigate challenges and uncertainties with confidence and determination, ultimately turning *no* into a powerful *yes*.

In the *Heart-Centered Approach*, authentic human connection is not an option – it is the heartbeat and pulse of organizational success. This strategy recognizes that the most powerful resource within any organization is its people. By authentically connecting with and supporting those individuals, a leader will unlock the full spectrum of human potential using leadership, energy, interaction, collaboration, and empathy. Leaders who prioritize authentic connections create workplaces where individuals thrive, innovate, and contribute their best.

Early on in my new HR career, I was asked not to blur the lines between personal and professional interactions, potentially undermining the seriousness of the workplace. However, keeping the personal and professional separate can hurt businesses. Life happens, and a leader's first step is understanding that work and life is an integration, not a balance.

♡ HEART TAKEAWAY

The *Heart-Centered Approach* does not mean sentimentality, softness, or ineffectiveness. It means fostering a positive workplace culture, building strong relationships, and simultaneously achieving both business goals as well as fostering an employee's goals for their own well-being. Leaders who embrace this approach see its value and understand how to strike a balance between empathy and productivity. You got this! In the next chapter we will talk about the pulse of every organization, and how a leader's heart makes the beat.

Heart-Centered ♡ Approach Story

A lot of life happens in 21 years. I was with Jo Ann longer than the 18 years I lived with my parents. Jo Ann *embraced* me in the cycle of life, such as: single, dating, engaged, married, pregnant, divorced, single motherhood, and dating again – and professionally, office drama and conflicts. For example, there were complaints that I was too loud (never quite had the *library voice*); I overextended my paid time off; and my favorite, my daughter Lauren starting a shaving cream fight while running around in the office. Jo Ann dealt with a lot – and had my back every time.

Looking back – how **did** she manage for 21 years – LOL simple – Jo Ann led with a *Heart-Centered Approach*: with compassion, empathy, and heart. Again, it is a choice. We may not have liked each other every day; however, we valued each other, respected each other, listened to each other, trusted each other, and were honest with one another each and every day.

Lastly, bravo to the leaders of the law firm who created a culture that allowed us to form friendships that now span over 30 years, and whom I now refer to as my Virginia Beach Tribe. My fondest memories are the sought-after Wimpy Award team-building events between the departments, holiday parties, lunch and learns, community-event walks, and King Neptune – always including a celebration!

Leadership and Organizational Culture

Take action, influence change, and inspire others to create a sense of purpose and direction.

This provides a positive organizational culture and boosts employee morale.

Chapter 2

Leadership, The Heartbeat of Success

Everything rises and falls on leadership...

—JOHN MAXWELL

Does Maxwell's quote resonate with your heartbeat? If it doesn't, you may need to check your vital signs, as leadership *is* the heartbeat of success in every organization – it can also be the death of one. Maxwell is 100% on point, as *everything* rises and falls on an organization's leadership. Keep in mind that leadership can emerge in various roles and does not restrict job titles or hierarchy on your organizational chart. Leaders are not only the owners, CEOs, presidents, board members, managers, supervisors, or HR professionals. Individuals in support roles demonstrate leadership qualities and responsibilities all day, every day.

For example: the receptionist. I believe this role is *the* heartbeat of success in an organization. The receptionist is the first impression and first point of contact for clients, customers, and visitors. Their professionalism, courtesy, and ability to handle inquiries all contribute to create a positive first impression, showcasing leadership in customer service. The receptionist also has to deal with unexpected situations daily, such as a difficult client or resolving a scheduling conflict, which requires quick thinking and effective problem-solving skills. A receptionist who communicates clearly, listens attentively, and conveys information accurately, contributes to the smooth functioning of the workplace. The receptionist should be at the *center* of every organizational chart, not the bottom.

I can go on and on about an organization's administrative support, frontline employees, and project team members, all who play a crucial role with: organization, confidentiality, taking initiative, customer interaction, team collaboration, adaptability, and accountability. Leadership is about the demonstration of qualities and behaviors that positively influence others and contribute to the success of the organization. Leadership is *not* a role, job title, or hierarchical position! Are you with me so far? Now that we have defined who a leader is in your organization, which is just about everyone, let me ask you:

- As the CEO, or a supervisor or manager, do you have a pulse on your employees?
- When was the last time you checked their heart rate or rhythm?
- Is there a continuous circulation of oxygen, or are there irregularities and disruptions?

Your employees are your organization's lifeblood. They are the very pulse that keeps an organization thriving, evolving, and growing. It is not only about quantitative metrics such as performance metrics, productivity, efficiency, and the financial health of an organization, but also the qualitative aspects, such as employee morale, communication channels, innovation, and creativity, that contribute to the overall well-being of the workplace. Just as a healthy pulse is fundamental for a thriving body, the employee's well-being, commitment, and engagement levels are the vital signs of an organization's overall health and vitality, providing insight into its culture, work environment, and employee morale.

At the heart of this discussion lies the question: What qualities must a leader embody to build trust, which is the essence of every successful organization? To answer this question Maxwell identifies three qualities a leader must demonstrate to build trust:

> *There are three qualities a leader*
> *must exemplify to build trust:*
> *competence, connection, and character.*
>
> —JOHN MAXWELL

1. **Competence:** It is the competent leader who paves the way for organizational success and long-term health. Competence refers to a wide range of attributes, from industry knowledge and technical expertise to problem-solving skills, effective decision-making, and delivering on commitments. A competent leader:

- Fosters a culture of innovation and creativity. This attitude inspires employees to think creatively, leading to a more dynamic and forward-thinking organization.
- Enables other leaders to approach issues and obstacles strategically to identify problems, assess root causes, and develop effective solutions. This problem-solving capability minimizes disruptions and ensures a smoother organizational operation.
- Attracts and retains top talent with their expertise and guidance, providing employees with valuable learning opportunities and contributing to professional development and career growth. This fosters a committed and high-performing workforce.
- Assesses the impact of external factors on the organization and pivots when necessary. Their ability to lead through change is fundamental in ensuring the organization's survival and growth.
- Makes sound, strategic decisions that align with the organization's mission and values. This, in turn, creates a sense of purpose and direction for employees, enhancing their commitment to the organization.

Competence in leadership is not just about one individual; it has a ripple effect throughout the organization. When a leader is competent, their team is more likely to emulate their behavior. However, incompetence at the highest levels can result in frustration, disengagement, and a lack of trust among employees. Incompetent leaders may make poor decisions, overlook critical details, and struggle to inspire their teams. Such situations can lead to high turnover, decreased morale, and a lack of direction, negatively impacting the organization's overall well-being. **Where are you on the path of a competent leader?**

2. **Connection:** A leader's ability to connect with their team nourishes the organization. Connection is more than mere interaction; it's the invisible thread that ties individuals together in trust, collaboration, and mutual understanding. When leaders take the time to listen, engage in meaningful conversations, and truly grasp the perspectives and feelings of their employees, a bond is created that is organically built on genuine care and concern.

When a leader values and exemplifies connection, it tends to influence the entire team, creating another rippling effect. Employees are more likely to adopt these values, fostering a culture of respect, empathy, and shared purpose. On the flip side, the absence of connection can result in low morale, distrust, and a fragmented work environment. Employees may feel isolated and disengaged, harming productivity and leading to higher turnover rates. These challenges can have detrimental consequences for the organization's overall health. **What are you doing to connect with your employees?**

3. **Character:** Character is not simply about doing what's right when convenient; it's about consistently adhering to ethical decision-making, even in the face of adversity, considering the welfare of the organization, its employees, and its stakeholders. It guides a leader's actions, decisions, and interactions with their team. Leaders with strong character demonstrate the following attributes:

Integrity and Honesty: These qualities form the basis of trust within an organization. When a leader consistently demonstrates these traits, it sends a powerful message to the team that ethical behavior and transparency are non-negotiable.

Resilience: Character instills resilience in leaders, enabling them to endure challenges and setbacks without compromising their ethical principles. Such leaders remain steadfast in their commitment to doing what's right, even when faced with adversity.

Accountability: Leaders who hold themselves accountable for their actions and are not afraid to take responsibility for both successes and failures set a standard within the organization and encourage employees to take ownership of their work.

Consistency: When leaders are consistent in their actions and decisions, predictability will foster a sense of security among employees. Such consistency promotes a stable work environment and reduces uncertainty.

Respect and Empathy: Leaders who embody these qualities create a culture of inclusivity and caring. Employees feel valued and appreciated, leading to improved job satisfaction.

The impact of a leader's character on organizational health leads to a workplace with high moral standards, a positive work environment, reputation, and long-term success and stability. When a leader's character is compromised, however, trust erodes leading to a decline in teamwork and performance. **What is the strength of your character?**

I don't think my friend John will mind if I add two more important leadership qualities that build trust.

4. Self-Awareness: When we are more self-aware of ourselves, we are able to see our lives through different lenses and perspectives of others. It provides us the opportunities to evaluate what should change, what new habits need to be formed, and how we envision our future. When we are more self-aware, it helps us to be more confident about who we are and what we are capable of; be better leaders and communicators; improve relationships and have higher levels of happiness; and, most importantly, navigate the complexity of human emotions.

Much like a mirror, which reflects our physical appearance, self-awareness reveals the inner aspects of leadership (reflecting one's true self, thoughts, emotions, and actions) that ultimately affect the health and success of an organization. Self-awareness allows leaders to understand their strengths, weaknesses, values, and their impact on others, which continually supports personal growth.

In essence, self-awareness provides a strong foundation for trust in leadership. Its absence can lead to poor decision-making, ineffective communication, reduced employee engagement, limited personal growth, trust issues, resistance to change, and a loss of credibility. **When was the last time you looked in the mirror? What did it reveal?**

Mirror, Mirror on the wall, who's the most self-aware of them all?

5. Heart of Gratitude: Having a heart of gratitude is a leader's genuine appreciation and thankfulness for the contributions of others. Leading with a heart of gratitude:

- Fosters trust by showing humility and appreciation for the collaborative efforts of their team.
- Creates a positive and motivating atmosphere within the organization, setting the tone for employees who will be more engaged and committed.
- Encourages a culture of recognition and mutual respect, reinforcing trustful relationships among team members.
- Contributes to the well-being of employees, feeling appreciated and valued, reducing stress, increasing job satisfaction, and fostering a sense of belonging.
- Enhances organizational performance where employees are inspired to excel, with leaders providing a continuous cycle of appreciation and acknowledging employee contributions.

Gratitude is the heart of effective leadership, fostering trust and driving success. When leaders cannot find the pulse of gratitude, negative adverse consequences will affect the organization, such as the ability to meet goals and objectives, complaints, dissatisfaction, and a focus on what's wrong rather than what's right. **Where is your heart of gratitude?**

Collectively, these five qualities of a leader: competence, connection, character, self-awareness, and heart of gratitude, contribute to the overall health and success of an organization by fostering trust, effective communication, and a positive organizational culture. A competent, connected, and ethical leader who practices self-awareness and gratitude can inspire and empower their team, ultimately leading to greater organizational achievements and well-being.

♡ HEART TAKEAWAY

1. Everyone in an organization has a leadership role.
2. An organization's success or failure is influenced by leadership.
3. The quality of the highest levels of leadership sets the tone for culture, engagement, innovation, and overall performance.
4. The importance of quantitative metrics and qualitative aspects.
5. There are five qualities a leader must embody to build trust.
6. Leadership is ultimately about taking action, influencing positive change, inspiring others, and creating a collective sense of purpose and direction. Your heartbeat will continue to be healthy because your organization is being led by employees who appreciate, trust, and recognize the efforts of those around them! You got this!

   In the next chapter, we will discuss how leaders focus on self-care, well-being, and wellness to make an impact on employees and the organization.

Heart-Centered ♡ Approach Story

Leaders have the power to light up a room with their words and actions. Each of us has the choice to break bad habits, create new good habits, and take an active role in what happens next! My friend, Annie Meehan, always shares that choices are made out of either love or fear. How we recover, and our resilience, is a mindset. Each choice also comes with accountability. Although we are free to choose, we are not free from the consequences of our choices – good, bad, or ugly. Have no regrets, though, because our choices are all lessons to learn. We need to hold ourselves accountable, accept the choices we make, and fill our hearts with gratitude.

Reminders:

1. We get to make choices on how we are going to live and show up every day.
2. We get to make choices on how we are going to bounce back.
3. We get to make choices in the effort to learn – to try again – and to be resilient!

Leaders... take action and light up the room!

Here is a story that I happened to see on a social media post, previously published in Art Lovers Welcome in 2022, that exemplifies this approach:

A professor gave a balloon to every student, who had to inflate it, write their name on it, and throw it into the hallway. The professor then mixed all the balloons. The students were then given five minutes to find their own balloon. Despite a hectic search, no one found their balloon.

At that point, the professor then asked the students to take the first balloon they found and hand it to the person whose name was written on it. Within five minutes, everyone had their own balloon.

The professor said to the students: these balloons are like happiness. We will never find it if everyone is looking for their own. But if we care about other people's happiness, we will find ours too.

Principle 3

Employee Well-Being

Foster a workplace culture where individuals feel valued, supported, and empowered to navigate the demands of work and life.

This leads to employees who are engaged, productive, and loyal to the organization.

Chapter 3

Wellness Wonderland: Cultivating Employee Well-Being

Almost everything will work again if you
unplug it for a few minutes – including you.

—ANNE LAMOTT, AUTHOR

Employee well-being and wellness are more than just buzzwords. They are the keys to a wellness wonderland – a place of magical adventures. Abracadabra leaders: it's showtime! The main attraction is understanding the benefits when cultivating employee well-being in your organization:

Enhances Productivity and Engagement: Well-being programs create a positive work environment where employees feel valued and supported, and thereby become more engaged, productive, and committed to their roles.

Attracts Top Talent and Improved Retention: Prioritizing employee well-being will appeal to job seekers, attracting and retaining top talent, as well as fostering employee loyalty, which reduces costs associated with recruiting and training new hires.

Creates Higher Morale and Job Satisfaction: A positive workplace culture emphasizing compassion, empathy, and heart as core values will contribute to a more inclusive, harmonious, and collaborative work environment.

Improves Health and Reduces Healthcare Costs: Wellness programs that promote regular exercise, balanced nutrition, preventive healthcare, and mental well-being initiatives will contribute to healthier employees: reducing stress, healthcare costs, absenteeism, and enhancing emotional resilience.

Increases Innovation and Creativity: Well-being initiatives that support an employee's sense of purpose will lower stress levels, inspiring them to seek new ways to contribute to the organization's success.

Understand that employee well-being is a shared responsibility between employers and employees. Well-being and wellness impact both employees and an organization's bottom line. However, in order to be effective leaders, we need to take care of ourselves first before we may effectively help anyone around us. Think about the last time you traveled on an airplane. What were the instructions if the oxygen masks dropped? You first, right? So, buckle up, as the next attraction in our wellness wonderland is to prioritize self-care. Self-Care serves as a foundation for effective leadership and organizational success.

Self-Care

Self-care has two parts: an organization's initiative, and employee choices to engage in self-care practices. Encouraging employees to incorporate self-care into their daily routines will have a profound impact on their overall well-being. Self-care practices may include:

- **Regular Exercise**, whether it's a daily walk, yoga, or gym session, promotes physical health and reduces stress.
- **Mindfulness and Relaxation** techniques, such as mindfulness, meditation, and deep breathing, can help manage stress and improve mental well-being.
- **Healthy Nutrition** and providing information about balanced diets and nutrition empowers employees to make healthier food choices.
- **Setting Boundaries** between work and personal life supports a healthy work-life integration.
- **Hobbies and Interests** that foster a sense of fulfillment and social well-being.
- **Seeking Support** to reach out for professional help when needed, whether it's for mental health counseling or financial advice, promotes overall well-being.

By promoting a culture of self-care in your organization, employees will feel seen, valued, empowered, and better equipped to navigate the demands of work and life. Organizations may contribute to a culture of self-care with:

- **Educational Initiatives:** Providing information and workshops on self-care practices.

- **Flexible Work Arrangements:** Offering flexibility in work hours or remote work to accommodate self-care activities.
- **Supportive Policies:** Creating policies that encourage work-life integration and self-care, such as generous paid time off (PTO) and mental health support.
- **Leading by Example:** Encouraging supervisors and managers to role model self-care behaviors, signaling its importance to the entire workforce.

What steps can you take in your organization to help promote self-care?

As we continue our magical adventure in our wellness wonderland, leaders should recognize that although well-being and wellness go hand-in-hand, it is important to not confuse the two. Employee well-being encompasses physical health, mental health, social connections, financial security, community, and a sense of purpose and fulfillment in both personal and work life. Wellness is breaking bad habits and practicing healthier ones.

Well-Being

Elevating your organization's well-being initiatives to meet the unique needs and preferences of your workforce will support the physical, mental, and emotional health of your employees. Here are some plans, services, and offers that you may consider:

Health Insurance Plans: A comprehensive health insurance plan typically covers a range of healthcare needs, including doctor visits, preventive care, prescriptions, emergency care, and treatments.

Employee Assistance Programs (EAPs): EAPs provide confidential counseling and support services to employees and their families for a wide range of personal and work-related issues, including stress, financial management, mental health, substance abuse, and family problems.

Paid Time Off (PTO): PTO includes various types of leave to meet an employee's needs, such as vacation, illness, professional development, bereavement, or inclement weather. PTO as part of an initiative recognizes the importance of rest and relaxation to maintain overall well-being.

Flexible Work Arrangements: Allow employees to have flexible work hours, remote work options, or compressed work weeks to improve a work-life integration and reduce stress.

Employee Recognition Programs: Recognize and reward employees for their contributions and achievements. Feeling valued and appreciated contributes to overall well-being.

Financial Benefits: Provide benefits such as retirement savings plans, life insurance, and disability coverage to ensure employees' financial security.

What well-being initiatives could fit into your organization's budget?

Wellness

Have fun and be creative when promoting wellness programs to engage employees. Here are some ideas:

Fitness Challenges: Organize fitness challenges such as step challenges, 5K races, or team-based competitions. Employees can track their progress and compete for prizes or recognition.

Wellness Bingo: Create a wellness bingo card with a variety of health and well-being activities, such as "Take a 10-minute stretch break" or "Try a new healthy recipe." Employees can mark off activities as they complete them and aim for bingo or other incentives.

Themed Dress-Up Days: Encourage employees to dress up according to fun and healthy themes, like "Sports Day," "Polka-Dot Day," or "Favorite Outdoor Activity Day." It adds a lighthearted touch to the workplace.

Healthy Recipe Contests: Host a healthy recipe contest where employees submit their favorite nutritious recipes. You can organize taste tests and award prizes for the most delicious and healthy dishes.

Meditation and Mindfulness Workshops, or Lunch and Learns: Offer meditation and mindfulness workshops led by experienced instructors. Employees can learn relaxation techniques and stress management strategies.

Wellness Webinars: Invite experts to conduct wellness webinars on topics like nutrition, fitness, mental health, and work-life balance. Employees can attend these informative sessions during breaks or after work.

Deskercise Challenges: Encourage employees to incorporate exercises into their workday. Provide a list of simple desk exercises, and employees can challenge themselves to complete them regularly.

Wellness Challenges with Wearable Tech: Many employees use fitness trackers or smartwatches. Organize wellness challenges that sync with these devices, allowing employees to compete or collaborate in achieving fitness goals.

Massage or Yoga Sessions: Arrange for on-site massage or yoga sessions during breaks or after work hours. Employees can relax and de-stress with these soothing activities.

Volunteer Opportunities: Encourage employees to participate in community service or volunteer projects as part of a wellness program. Giving back can boost a sense of purpose and well-being.

What creative and unique wellness programs will fit your culture?

Remember that the effectiveness of well-being and wellness programs depends on employee engagement and participation. Offering a variety of fun attractions and exciting rides in your organization's wonderland can encourage employees to take an active interest in their well-being. Regular evaluation and feedback from employees can help refine and improve these programs over time.

♡ HEART TAKEAWAY

Remind yourself to unplug first so you may help those around you. By providing well-being initiatives and wellness programs in your organization, you will empower employees to take ownership of their well-being. Remember, these components are interconnected as a partnership between employers and employees, with each playing a vital role in your organization's wellness wonderland. You got this! The next chapter will focus on how to engage with your employees. Continue to smile and keep an open mind as you continue to *Lead with Love.*

Heart-Centered 💜 Approach Story

Allow me to introduce you to my soul sister, Kim, President of Kim LaMontagne, LLC, an expert on wellbeing and mental health in the workplace. Kim's story is one of strength, self-awareness, resilience, and bravery.

Kim LaMontagne's Story

This is the story about a conversation that changed **and saved** my life. I was a high performing professional, and I suffered (in silence) with depression, anxiety, alcohol misuse, and intense suicidal thoughts. On spreadsheets and reports, I appeared to be stellar, fearless, and unstoppable. Behind the mask of performance, I felt like an imposter, feared judgment, retribution, job loss, being seen as weak and incapable, and damaging my professional integrity if I spoke openly and acknowledged that I needed help. As a result, I remained silent my entire corporate career, and almost lost my life.

In 2016, an observant leader noticed the subtle signs that something was wrong and took action. She scheduled a field visit with me, flew from New Jersey to Massachusetts, conducted one sales call, created a safe space, and asked if **I was truly ok**. For the first time, I felt safe to open up and speak my truth. She was stunned by what I shared, practiced empathy, and was very supportive. She asked how I had been operating at such high levels with such pain going on in the background.

My response was simple: Fear and shame.

My leader gave me extra time off around Memorial Day weekend, and that is when my healing journey began. Now, I teach leaders to do what my leader did, to see the signs and take action.

In 2020, I stepped away from my corporate role, created Kim LaMontagne, LLC, and launched my corporate training program called, "The 4 Pillars of Creating a Mentally Healthy Workplace." The goal of "The 4 Pillars" is to teach leaders how to create a culture of safety, where everyone feels safe asking for help, without fear of judgment, retribution, or job loss. Leaders are not counselors, but they are the first line of defense and have the power to transform the workplace.

At 14 years sober and healthy, I share my lived experience and train leaders how to navigate the conversation about mental health, recognize the signs, open a safe dialogue, decrease stigma, shift to person-centered language, harness the power of peer support, and create a culture of safety in the workplace. I have the unique ability to teach through the lens of lived experience and the lens of the leader. I have worked with clients in healthcare, education, legal, corporate, construction, HR, and non-profit; and am a frequent Keynote Speaker. What I know to be true is, we are not alone, our mental health matters, and we must train leaders to normalize the conversation about mental health in the workplace. Lives depend on it.

One in five people live (and work) with a mental health condition. Are you and your leaders prepared to see the signs, open a safe dialogue, and crosswalk an employee to services? If you're unsure, you are not alone. Many leaders report feeling unprepared to open the dialogue about mental health because they haven't been trained or don't know what to say. Consequently, many conversations are still being avoided.

My leader saved my life and she didn't even know it. She simply noticed the signs and had the conversation with me that changed (and saved) my life.

Principle 4
Employee Engagement

Nurture ongoing employee engagement efforts to boost positive outcomes for an organization's success.

This creates enthusiastic contributors who will provide better service and innovative solutions.

Chapter 4

The Secret to Employee Engagement

When people go to work, they shouldn't
have to leave their hearts at home.

—BETTY BENDER

Take a moment and sit with each of these questions:

- Do you expect dedication from your employees?
- Do you want to improve your bottom line?
- Do you want to be respected as a leader?

Presuming you answered *yes* to each of these questions, it's time to make an impact on employee engagement with the *Heart-Centered Approach*. If you answered *no*, calmly put the book down and call me right away, as this is an emergency situation. Your heart may have just stopped beating!

True engagement goes beyond merely showing up, fulfilling job responsibilities, and collecting a paycheck. Employees are holistic beings with emotions, values, and passions that are integral to their identity. In the context of the workplace, recognizing employees as holistic beings means acknowledging they bring their complete selves to work, including their emotions, values, beliefs, and personal experiences, and all these elements influence their engagement and performance. Long gone are the days of employees checking their hearts at the door like their personal lives don't matter. Because it *all* matters, and is the secret sauce of employee engagement.

Leaders must recognize that employees are not all created equal, and that employee engagement is not a one-size-fits-all concept. It encompasses a wide range of emotions, attitudes, and behaviors that reflect how employees relate to their work and their organization. Once leaders understand this and allow employees to bring their whole selves to work, including their hearts, it leads to several key outcomes that benefit your bottom line:

Emotional Connection: Employees who feel that their emotions, values, and personal beliefs are welcomed at work are more likely to form a deep emotional connection with their organization. This can drive higher levels of engagement when employees genuinely care about an organization's mission, values, and goals, and if they understand how their roles contribute to the organization's success and are dedicated to achieving it. *Engaged employees speak positively about their organization, both within and outside the workplace, and are brand advocates, contributing to a positive organizational reputation.*

Intrinsic Motivation: Allowing employees to express their authentic selves at work can tap into their intrinsic motivation, referring to an employee's internal drive or desires. When employees can align their personal values and passions with their job roles, they are more likely to find fulfillment in their work, driving higher levels of engagement and commitment. *Engaged employees are self-motivated and take initiative in their work. They are driven by a sense of purpose and personal satisfaction in their contributions.*

Creativity and Innovation: When employees are encouraged to bring their hearts to work, it fosters an environment where diverse perspectives, creative thinking, and innovative ideas can flourish. Engagement levels tend to rise when employees feel empowered to contribute their unique insights and talents. *Engaged employees are proactive in finding solutions to challenges and improving processes, consistently striving for excellence in their roles.*

Stronger Team Dynamics: Encouraging employees to bring their hearts to work promotes a culture of authenticity and trust. This, in turn, leads to stronger team relationships, as individuals are more open and empathetic. High levels of trust and positive team dynamics are closely linked to engagement. *Engaged employees work well with others, support their colleagues, and foster a sense of community.*

Well-Being and Resilience: Recognizing and valuing the emotional well-being of employees is a key aspect of the *Heart-Centered Approach*, which was discussed in the last chapter. When employees are encouraged to address their emotional needs and well-being, they are more likely to experience a sense of balance and resilience, which can positively impact their engagement and overall job satisfaction. *Engaged employees are more* *resilient in the face of challenges and setbacks. They approach difficulties with a positive attitude and a determination to overcome them.*

The *Heart-Centered Approach* provides a powerful framework for nurturing and sustaining employees so that they are engaged. Leaders play a pivotal role in shaping the employee experience and influencing engagement levels. We discussed this in-depth in Chapter 2. Heart-centered leadership involves leading by example and modeling the behavior and attitudes you wish to see in your teams. When team leaders exhibit passion, dedication, and a commitment to the organization's values, they inspire trust, loyalty, and commitment among their teams. To effectively apply the *Heart-Centered Approach* to employee engagement, organizations and leaders should focus on the following strategies and best practices:

Open and Transparent Communication

Effective communication is the heartbeat of employee engagement. Open and transparent communication channels provide employees with the information they need to understand the organization's goals, changes, and expectations. It also creates an environment where employees feel comfortable sharing their ideas and concerns. When difficult choices are necessary and leaders communicate openly and transparently, this will demonstrate empathy and understanding.

Best Practices:

Active Listening: Actively listening to employees, being present (no other distractions), and seeking to understand their concerns, aspirations, and feedback creates a sense of belonging and shows that employees' voices are valued.

Regular Updates: Provide regular updates on organizational goals, performance, and changes. This keeps employees informed and engaged in the company's journey.

Two-Way Communication: Encourage two-way communication channels that allow employees to ask questions, provide feedback, and share their insights. Actively respond to their inquiries and concerns.

Storytelling: Share compelling stories that illustrate the organization's values and successes. Stories create a sense of purpose and help employees connect emotionally with the company's mission.

Transparency: Be transparent about the organization's challenges and opportunities. Transparency builds trust and demonstrates authenticity.

Recognition and Appreciation

Recognition is a powerful driver of employee engagement. When employees feel their contributions are acknowledged and appreciated, they are more likely to remain engaged and motivated. Annual reviews are not enough. Heart-centered recognition goes beyond monetary rewards and includes personal gestures that convey genuine appreciation.

Best Practices:

Timely Recognition: Recognize and appreciate employees' efforts promptly and publicly. Timely recognition reinforces positive behaviors and encourages continued excellence.

Peer-to-Peer Recognition: Encourage peer-to-peer recognition programs that allow employees to acknowledge their colleagues' contributions. Peer recognition promotes a sense of camaraderie and teamwork.

Personalized Recognition: Tailor recognition efforts to individual preferences. Some employees may prefer public recognition, while others may appreciate private, one-on-one appreciation.

Celebrating Milestones: Celebrate personal and professional milestones with employees. Recognize birthdays, work anniversaries, and other significant achievements to show that you care about their well-being.

Personal Growth and Development

Supporting employees' personal growth and development is **essential** for maintaining high levels of engagement. Engaged employees are often those who see opportunities for advancement, learning, and skill development within their roles. Help employees grow or watch them go! This one strategy alone will take an organization to a whole new level!

Best Practices:

Individual Development Plans: Work with employees to create individual development plans that align with their career aspirations and the organization's needs.

Skill-Building Opportunities: Provide access to training, workshops, and learning resources that allow employees to acquire new skills and knowledge.

Mentorship Programs: Establish mentorship programs that pair experienced employees with those looking to develop their skills and advance their careers.

Feedback and Growth Discussions: Hold regular feedback and growth discussions with employees to assess their progress, identify areas for improvement, and set goals for personal and professional development.

Well-Being and Work-Life Integration

Employees who feel their well-being is valued are more likely to remain engaged and committed to their work, which we discussed extensively in Chapter 3. Promoting a healthy work-life integration and offering well-being programs demonstrates the organization's concern for employees' physical and mental health and what happens AFTER 5:00 PM.

Best Practices:

> **Flexible Work Arrangements:** Provide flexible work arrangements, such as remote work options or flexible hours, to accommodate employees' personal needs and responsibilities.

> **Mental Health Support:** Offer mental health resources, such as counseling services, stress management workshops, and access to mindfulness programs.

> **Wellness Programs:** Implement wellness programs that promote physical health, including fitness challenges, nutrition guidance, and access to fitness facilities.

> **Stress Reduction:** Create a stress-free workplace by fostering a culture that encourages breaks, relaxation, and stress-reduction activities.

Employee Involvement and Decision-Making

Engaged employees are often those who have a say in decisions that affect their work. Managers and supervisors should consider encouraging employee feedback when new decisions are made or considered for departments; involving employees in decision-making processes not only increases their engagement but also leads to better, more informed choices. Also, leaders should consider the impact of their decisions on employees.

Best Practices:

Employee Surveys: Conduct regular surveys to gather employees' opinions and suggestions on various aspects of the organization, from workplace policies to strategic decisions.

Cross-Functional Teams: Form cross-functional teams that include employees from different departments to collaborate on projects and strategic initiatives.

Task Forces: Establish task forces or working groups dedicated to specific challenges or opportunities, allowing employees to contribute their expertise.

Employee Resource Groups: Encourage the formation of employee resource groups (ERGs) that focus on diversity, inclusion, and shared interests. ERGs provide a platform for employees to have a voice in shaping the organization's culture and practices.

Measuring and Tracking Engagement

To nurture and sustain employee engagement effectively, organizations must have reliable methods for measuring and tracking it. Regular assessments allow leaders to identify areas for improvement and gauge the effectiveness of engagement initiatives.

Best Practices:

Employee Surveys: Use employee engagement surveys to collect feedback and assess engagement levels. Ensure that survey questions are designed to capture the various dimensions of engagement, including commitment, motivation, and well-being.

Pulse Surveys: Conduct periodic pulse surveys to gather quick, real-time feedback on specific issues or initiatives. Pulse surveys help organizations stay responsive to employees' changing needs.

Exit/Stay Interviews: Analyze feedback from exit interviews to identify patterns or trends related to disengagement and turnover. Use this information to make targeted improvements. Also, including stay interviews will help organizations discover what employees value about their roles and what can be improved before they exit.

Performance Metrics: Monitor key performance indicators (KPIs) related to productivity, turnover rates, and employee satisfaction. Changes in these metrics can provide insights into the impact of engagement efforts.

♡ HEART TAKEAWAY

Nurturing employee engagement with the *Heart-Centered Approach* is a journey that requires dedication, commitment, and ongoing effort. Focusing on employee engagement and implementing these best practices helps organizations to create an environment where employees are not only productive workers, but they are also enthusiastic contributors who are deeply engaged in their roles and invested in the success of the organization for positive outcomes:

- Increased engagement with a notable boost in motivation, commitment, and well-being indicators.
- Decreased turnover rates, resulting in cost savings associated with recruitment and onboarding.
- Empowered employees who contribute their ideas and take ownership of their projects, resulting in increased productivity and innovation.
- Engaged employees who provide better service and develop innovative solutions to meet client needs, resulting in higher customer satisfaction.

Heart-Centered ♡ Approach Story

I am one of those happy people with contagious energy, who leads with the *Heart-Centered Approach*. The world does not always welcome or appreciate people like me. For so long, I thought I was doing it wrong. I did not understand how bringing energy into a room, being happy, and leading with a *Heart-Centered Approach* were bad things.

Then, I read *The Four Agreements* by Don Miguel Ruiz. This book helped me realize it was okay to be me. One of the companies I worked with gave this book to each client. I will be forever grateful for the introduction to it. I check in with myself on these four agreements daily, and also provide workshops and leadership training on these.

The Four Agreements are:

1 **Be Impeccable with Your Word:** Speak with integrity. Say only what you mean. Avoid using words to speak against yourself or to gossip about others. Use the power of your word to offer love, never use it to cause fear or pain in another (or yourself).

2 **Always Do Your Best:** Your best is going to change from moment to moment; it will be different when you are healthy as opposed to sick. Under any circumstance, simply do your best, and you will avoid self-judgment, self-abuse, and regret.

3 **Don't Make Assumptions:** Find the quiet courage to ask questions and to express what you really want. Communicate with others as clearly as you can to avoid misunderstandings, sadness, and drama. With just this one agreement, you can completely transform your life.

4 **Don't Take Anything Personally:** Nothing others do is because of you. What others say and do is a result of their own dream or perception of their rules. We all make rules about how things should be; but when you are immune to the opinions and actions of others, you won't be the victim of needless suffering.

Growing up in Cleveland, Ohio, my parents provided me with a solid foundation of lots of love, belief in myself, and faith. I was a fortunate child. The baby of four, I was spoiled. My father was a Holocaust survivor and lost his family during that time period. I share this with you because I always felt that if my father could bear such devastation and horror, and could still be happy and smiling, and have a giving heart, and love everyone no matter what walk of life they came from, what did I have to complain about and judge?!

I certainly learned early on that there were no obstacles, risks, or mistakes that I could not turn into opportunities. You see, the *Heart-Centered Approach* is a mindset – a way of life – an inside job. We had a round kitchen table to seat the six of us. My mother always said if everyone could sit around our table, and we would all put our troubles in the middle, we would want our troubles back because someone always had it worse. You never know what someone's story is or in what chapter they are. Always *Lead with Love.*

Once I climbed that organizational chart, and left Jo Ann's *cocoon* of the *Heart-Centered Approach* after 21 years, and was provided new opportunities to lead with it, I actually struggled to find a place where my values and my heart aligned. In spite of the foundation provided to me by my parents, Mr. Bobowick, and Jo Ann, I began to doubt myself. At each company, my *Heart-Centered Approach* was misunderstood, undervalued, and underappreciated, which led to separations, some mutual and some not so much. Not once, however, did I ever feel like I failed or was defeated because I was staying true to who I am with my beliefs and my values.

Leaders – listen up – long gone are the days of leaving our personal problems at the door and maintaining a distance from employees because of where you are on the organizational chart. Consistently through my HR career, I was asked to keep my personal and professional life separate – had to lead on a strict hierarchy and authoritarian leadership style – and employee friendships were discouraged.

Policies are *NOT* one-size-fits all!

Performance Reviews are *NOT* an annual event!

HR is *NOT* a reactive function or department!

Be *a CEO, a manager, a supervisor, or an employee with leadership potential* who values individuality, well-being, and the holistic development of employees. I assure you, by adopting a *Heart-Centered Approach* that aligns with your organization's mission, vision, and strategic plan, your strict dress code and rigid work hours will not be needed because your teams and employees will be taking care of you, your customers, and your bottom line, achieving organizational success.

Recruitment and Onboarding

Attract top talent who possess the required expertise and soft skills, and who align with the organizational culture. Provide comprehensive orientation, training, and a welcoming environment.

This ensures new employees are well-prepared and motivated to contribute effectively to the organization's success.

Chapter 5

You Had Me at Hello: Recruitment and Onboarding

I'd rather interview 50 people and not hire anyone than hire the wrong person.

—JEFF BEZOS

Jeff Bezos, founder of Amazon, understands the cascading effect a poor hire can have. Does this sound crazy, daunting, time-consuming, or resource-intensive? It may be; however, good hiring practices are one of the most critical investments an organization can make to secure its future success, growth, culture, and bottom line. Here are some key ways a poor hire can negatively affect an organization:

Pitfalls of Hasty Hires

Decreased Productivity and Employee Engagement: A poor hire may struggle to perform their job effectively, leading to decreased productivity. This not only affects their own work but can also create bottlenecks in processes and projects; and not only reduces the overall productivity of their team, but also potentially impacts other teams as well. A poor hire can contribute to a decrease in overall engagement, affecting the organization's ability to retain top talent.

Increased Costs: Recruiting and onboarding a new employee involves significant costs, including advertising, interviewing, training, and administrative expenses. When a poor hire doesn't work out, these costs are essentially wasted, and the organization may need to incur additional expenses to find a replacement. And, if the poor hire is not addressed promptly, it may lead to increased turnover within the organization. High turnover is costly in terms of recruitment, onboarding, and lost institutional knowledge.

Negative Impact on Morale: The presence of a poor hire can demoralize the rest of the team. Co-workers may need to pick up the slack for the underperforming employee, leading to frustration, burnout, and decreased job satisfaction. This can result in higher turnover rates as well.

Damage to Customer Relationships: In customer-facing roles, a poor hire can damage relationships with clients or customers. Mistakes, unprofessional behavior, or a lack of expertise can lead to customer complaints, loss of business, and a tarnished reputation.

Cultural Erosion: An organization's culture is built on shared values, behaviors, and norms. A poor hire who does not align with the organization's culture can disrupt the harmony within the organization (as can a candidate who realizes they do not not align with the organization early on and leaves; remember, this is a two-way street). This may lead to conflicts, disengagement, and a decline in employee morale.

Increased Workload for Management: Managers may need to invest a disproportionate amount of time and effort in managing and coaching a poor hire. This diverts their attention from other important responsibilities and can hinder their ability to lead effectively.

Missed Opportunities and Strategic Delays: A poor hire may not be capable of recognizing and capitalizing on opportunities for innovation, growth, or improvement. This can result in missed opportunities that could have otherwise benefited the organization. Also, if a poor hire is in a critical role, it can delay the execution of strategic initiatives, affecting the organization's ability to achieve its long-term goals. And, do not automatically presume a critical role means the CEO. For example, the receptionist who answers your phones is just as critical.

Legal and Compliance Risks: Depending on the nature of the role, a poor hire may not adhere to legal and compliance requirements, potentially exposing the organization to legal risks, fines, or reputational damage. Unfortunately, I see this often with managers and supervisors who are not trained and refuse to seek out human resources or an employment law attorney for guidance.

Impact on an Organization's Reputation: In the age of social media and online reviews, an organization's reputation can be easily tarnished by negative employee experiences. A poor hire's negative feedback or public departure can impact how the organization is perceived by potential employees and customers.

To mitigate these risks, organizations should invest in robust recruitment and onboarding processes that focus on finding candidates who not only possess the necessary technical skills, which are job-specific and related to expertise, but also, and more importantly, the soft skills that align with the organization's values and culture. Unlike a candidate's technical skills, learned through training or education, soft skills refer to a candidate's character traits, learned through personal experiences, that are developed over time.

Sir Richard Branson, founder of the Virgin Group, feels the most important factor in building his team is personality, which takes precedence over a technical skill set. Why are soft skills more appealing? Because you can't train attitude and personality, but you can train technical skills.

> *Hire character.*
> *Train skill.*
> —PETER SCHUTZ, FORMER PRESIDENT AND CEO OF PORSCHE AG

Soft Skills

Some common examples of soft skills include:

Communication: The ability to express ideas, thoughts, and information clearly and effectively through verbal, non-verbal, and written communication, active listening, and adaptability. Strong communication skills can minimize misunderstandings, deliver a persuasive presentation, and empathetically address concerns.

Teamwork: The capacity to collaborate and work cooperatively with others to achieve common goals and objectives. Those who excel at teamwork not only bring their expertise to the table, but also empower and support their teammates. They recognize that together, the team can achieve more than the sum of individual contributions, creating a synergistic work environment where everyone thrives.

Networking: Building and maintaining relationships with individuals and professionals to exchange information and opportunities. Those skilled in networking recognize that the connections they cultivate today may lead to collaborative projects, mentorship, or career advancements in the future. It's a strategic soft skill that expands horizons and opens doors to new possibilities.

Problem-Solving: The capability to identify, analyze, and find solutions to complex problems or challenges. Problem solvers exhibit creativity and resourcefulness, thinking outside the box to tackle issues from various angles. They are persistent and adaptable, viewing setbacks as opportunities to learn and refine their problem-solving skills.

Critical Thinking: The skill of evaluating information, ideas, and situations in a logical and analytical manner to make informed decisions. Critical thinkers are curious, inquisitive, and willing to challenge assumptions. This is a key soft skill that helps individuals contribute to better problem-solving and strategic planning within an organization.

Attitude: An individual's outlook, perspective, and overall demeanor towards tasks, challenges, and interactions with others. A positive attitude involves optimism, resilience, and a proactive approach to problems. It can greatly influence how one handles adversity, approaches new opportunities, and interacts with colleagues.

Enthusiasm: A measure of one's passion, energy, and excitement for their work, projects, or goals. It often results in increased motivation, creativity, and a willingness to go the extra mile. Enthusiastic individuals tend to inspire and motivate their colleagues, fostering a more dynamic and engaged team environment.

Professionalism: Professionalism encompasses a range of behaviors and attributes that reflect a high level of competence, integrity, and ethical conduct in the workplace. It involves qualities such as punctuality, reliability, accountability, and respect for colleagues and organizational policies.

What is the lesson on recruiting so far? Don't hire to fill a seat and do a job! The days of slotting individuals into roles solely based on qualifications are dwindling. Recruitment today is like the quest for the perfect puzzle piece – one that not only fits the position but seamlessly integrates into the organizational mosaic. It is a blend of values, work styles, and expectations.

The Recruiting Process

To provide a comprehensive understanding of recruitment, we will start by explaining the steps involved in the process:

Define your Brand: The first step in successful recruitment is defining your brand and creating a workplace culture that magnetizes the right individuals. Organizations with vibrant, inclusive cultures naturally attract skilled candidates. Prospective employees are no longer merely seeking paychecks – they yearn for workplaces that foster growth, inclusion, and purpose.

Identify the Need: This need can arise from various factors, including growth, turnover, or the creation of a new position. By conducting a thorough gap analysis (comparing an actual performance with a potential or desired performance) as part of the need identification process, organizations can make informed decisions about when, where, and how to recruit to address workforce deficiencies effectively. This strategic approach helps ensure that recruitment efforts are aligned with the organization's overarching goals and are tailored to meet specific talent needs.

Conduct a Job Analysis: A thorough job analysis defines the roles and responsibilities of the position in question. This step involves gathering information about the job's duties, required skills, qualifications, salary range, and reporting structure.

Create a Job Description: A detailed job description is an internal, comprehensive document that outlines the essential functions, such as type of job, job title, location, qualifications, KSAs (Knowledge, Skills, and Abilities), experience and education, and responsibilities of the position. It serves as a critical tool for both the recruitment and onboarding processes.

Develop a Job Posting: A job posting is an external, **brief,** and attention-grabbing advertisement highlighting the most important aspects of the job. The key word here is brief! A job posting is not the job description. Candidates sometimes do not get past the search for the role they are seeking. Understand it is a marketing tool to attract qualified candidates that showcases the job's benefits and opportunities.

Application Screening: This step is the most time consuming and involves reviewing the applications and resumes submitted by the candidates, assessing whether the applicants meet the minimum qualifications and requirements specified in the job description, thereby narrowing down the pool of candidates.

Selection: Candidates who pass the initial screening are further evaluated to determine their suitability for the role. This includes a phone screening, an interview, assessment(s), and reference checks. Selection methods may vary depending on the organization and specific job; but the goal is to assess and identify the top candidates who are the best fit for the organization. Do not let a great candidate slip through your fingertips because of organizational delays, such as the need to go through a chain of interviews. A great candidate will not wait for you.

Hiring: Once the selection process is complete, the organization should extend a formal job offer to the chosen candidate. An Offer Letter should include the following:

- Job Title
- Name of Immediate Supervisor

- Start Date
- Whether the position is full-time or part-time
- Classification: Exempt or Nonexempt
- Compensation
- Hours of employment
- Wage payment schedule
- Benefits
- At-Will language
- Statement subject to I-9 documentation, as well as any other contingencies, such as background checks and/or drug tests
- Require the employee to sign and date the Offer Letter acknowledging the terms

Background Checks: Please – Do not – Miss – This – Step! Once the signed Offer Letter is returned, do your due diligence and partner with a third party who offers this service. You will not only improve the quality of hires, but you will also protect your employees, customers, the organization's reputation and prevent possible theft or other criminal activity. We will discuss the importance of a background check more in Chapter 10.

A note on hiring a candidate with a record: Remember, lead with the *Heart-Centered Approach*, and recognize that not all arrests lead to a conviction. Talk to the candidate with empathy, and believe in the power of second chances. I understand not all industries can hire a second-chance candidate; however, if you can, I challenge you to have an open mind. Visit https://www.us-chamber.com to read about the benefits of second-chance hiring.

You will learn that individuals with a criminal record perform the same as or better than employees without criminal records.

Recruitment Methods

How do you find quality candidates? It is common for organizations to use a combination of methods to attract and hire top candidates. Here is a list of sourcing methods:

1. **Job Postings:** Posting job openings on the organization's website, job boards, and social media platforms.

2. **Employee Referrals:** Encouraging current employees to refer candidates for open positions. Some organizations provide a bonus after the referral stays a period of time (i.e. 90 days).

3. **Internal Promotions:** Identifying and promoting existing employees to fill vacant roles.

4. **Outsourcing Recruitment Agencies:** Engaging third-party recruitment agencies to find and vet candidates. This can be a huge timesaver for the organization.

5. **Temporary Staffing:** Using temporary staffing agencies to fill short-term or project-based positions.

6. **Networking and Professional Associations:** Leveraging personal and professional networks and engaging with professional associations relevant to the industry can help connect and identify potential candidates.

7. **Job Fairs:** Participating in or hosting job fairs and career expos to meet and interview candidates.

8. **Internship Programs:** Offering internship programs that can lead to full-time employment for successful interns.

The choice of a recruitment method will depend on factors such as the nature of the job, the desired candidate pool, budget constraints, and the organization's overall recruitment strategy. Please keep in mind, automation should not replace the *human* element of recruiting. Artificial Intelligence (AI) is not new: ChatGPT has just become popular and has now changed the landscape of the organization's recruitment processes, especially with writing job descriptions and job postings.

Here are two great examples of AI and automation: one leads with the *Heart-Centered Approach,* and the other is a fantastic ah-hah moment:

Heart-Centered Approach

A friend in Naples, Florida, who owns a dry cleaning business, recently automated one of their processes to modernize their business. This one automation previously took two employees to do this task. Instead of eliminating the two employees, they were moved to other roles. Bravo!

An Ah-Hah Moment

A client recently shared their frustration about new hires that were not understanding the expectations of the organization. Since their onboarding process is automated online, I asked if anyone had met with the new hires after completing the automated onboarding process. The answer was no – and the solution was simple with a high-five celebration. *Solution: take time to meet with each new hire and go over the Employee Handbook and share with them the organization's mission, values, and expectations.*

AI and automation can certainly contribute to increased efficiency, precision, and productivity. It also has the potential to analyze vast amounts of data quickly, leading to better decision-making and problem-solving. However, the data is only as good as the input. Therefore, you cannot rely on it completely. Organizations need to recognize how they can benefit the most when it comes to using AI or *human* intelligence. When implemented with a *Heart-Centered Approach*, AI and automation can be a valuable tool for the recruitment process.

Reflect: When was the last time *you* went through a job search? How did you feel? Did the rejections weigh on your psyche? You never know when *you* may find yourself in that same situation. Keep in mind that we never know what someone's story is. Therefore, lead with the *Heart-Centered Approach* in your recruitment efforts. Remember, a job seeker is a human with a heart. Processes and systems are necessary; however, we don't need to create additional anxiety for the job seeker and make them wait weeks for an interview – or never get back to them after taking the time to meet the candidate. Be clear, transparent, and human.

Onboarding

"You had me at hello," is a famous line that Renee Zellweger said to Tom Cruise in the 1996 film, *Jerry McGuire*. It means, "I found you irresistible from our first introduction." This is onboarding. Although onboarding is part of the process, it should be an experience for the new hire. Onboarding is an organization's opportunity to win the heart of the new hire, giving them a warm welcome and showing them they belong.

Onboarding is the last step in the recruitment process, and has a significant impact on the new hire's perception of the organization's culture. Onboarding should be a top priority in any organization. A successful onboarding experience:

- sets the stage for long-term success
- reduces the time it takes for new hires to become productive contributors
- enhances employee retention by helping newcomers feel connected and valued

One misconception of onboarding is that leaders believe it starts on a new hire's first day of employment. The fact is, the period between accepting a job offer and the first day can be filled with anticipation and excitement for the new employee. Use this time to build on their enthusiasm. A warm welcome email or letter that expresses the organization's excitement about their upcoming arrival is an example of leading with the *Heart-Centered Approach*. Maybe even send some swag!

Other pre-boarding helpful suggestions are:

- reduce administrative tasks and email the necessary forms and paperwork ahead of time
- set up any technology and equipment in advance to allow the employee to hit the ground running, making the first day productive
- connect the current team and new hire with a virtual introduction
- clarify expectations such as dress code, parking arrangements, and schedule

- encourage the new hire to reach out with any questions or concerns before their start date and begin the important open lines of communication

Training is not an option, it is a necessity

Imagine... you hired the perfect candidate. They checked every box on your wishlist, from skill sets to experience and education. They passed the background screening *and* drug test. You may be thinking that minimal training will suffice. But your perfect candidate still needs to be trained. Effective training is a fundamental aspect of onboarding. Just because your dream candidate knows how to do the skill, do they know how to do it for *you*? If you want to retain that perfect new employee, and have them live up to your expectations, you must provide the information, resources, and help in order for them to do their job successfully.

This includes:

- customized training to accommodate individual needs, preferences, and backgrounds
- a structured orientation to provide an introduction to the organization and co-workers, important processes and procedures, and databases
- an assigned mentor to guide and support the new hire during their transition
- access to the necessary resources and tools needed to excel in their roles
- a clear process for open communication and feedback, including a safe place for the new hire to ask questions without worry of judgment

The consequences of not training, and throwing your new, prized employee into the deep end will have detrimental effects on the workforce, the organization's overall performance, and a negative reputation for the leader. Inadequate training will lead to inefficiencies, errors, and lower productivity. The new employee will feel unsupported, frustrated, and disengaged, leading to turnover, dissatisfaction, and negative customer experiences. Ultimately, this could lead to loss of business, or worse yet, increased risk of employment-related litigation. Your dream hire just turned into a nightmare.

Are you awake yet? Yes? Good – because not having the proper onboarding documents is just as scary as not training properly. There are three types of onboarding documents: legal, job and organization-specific, and payroll and benefits.

Legal Documents (Required):

- W-4 Form: Required tax document to determine taxes withheld on each paycheck.
- I-9 Form: It is the employer's responsibility to verify that each candidate is eligible to work based on their citizenship, visa, resident, or immigration status. If you don't, serious fines and penalties may be assessed. Note: if you have an organization with 25 or more employees, you must also E-Verify. Visit https://www.e-verify.gov for more information.

Job and Organization-Specific Documents (Highly Recommended):

- Employment Offer Letter (discussed above)
- Confidentiality Agreement: Provides legal protection and requirements to keep intellectual property confidential.
- Equipment Receipt Form: Helps organizations document issuance of equipment, keys, etc.
- Employee Information Form (with Emergency Contact Information): Useful for a quick reference for basic employee data, including an emergency contact.
- Organizational Chart: Although I am not a fan, they are necessary to assist employees in understanding an organization's structure, hierarchy, and reporting relationships.
- Employee Handbook: A one-stop shop for information and protection. If it were up to me, a Handbook would be a requirement instead of an option; that is how critical a Handbook is. An Employee Handbook:
  » introduces employees to your culture, mission, and values
  » communicates expectations and promotes open communication
  » educates employees on best practices, logistics, and entitlements
  » explains an organization's policies and procedures
  » showcases benefits offered, such as holidays, time off, and insurance

» ensures compliance with federal and state laws

» protects organizations against any employee claims

» provides employees direction to obtain workplace-related help

All it takes is *one* employee to cause the Department of Labor to come knocking. When they do (*not if*), the first thing they will ask for is a copy of your Handbook. If you don't have one, get your checkbook out, as it will cost you a lot more than the cost to prepare a Handbook. Create a Handbook and review it at least annually.

Payroll and Benefits Documents (Helpful):

- Direct Deposit Authorization Form: Collects bank account information for processing payments
- Benefit Forms or Guide: Details the organization's benefits, including, but not limited to, medical insurance, retirement plans, and, if offered, life insurance

♡ HEART TAKEAWAY

Take a breath. I know this was a lot of information on recruitment and onboarding to take in. The *Heart Takeaways* are to remember recruitment involves attracting and selecting top talent who not only possess the required skills, but also align with the organization's culture and values. Onboarding, on the other hand, is the bridge that transforms new hires into engaged and productive employees when you provide comprehensive orientation, complete training, and a welcoming environment, ensuring they feel well-prepared and motivated to contribute effectively to the organization's success. You got this! In the next Chapter we will talk about how you *keep* your employees... and if you can't keep them... best practices on saying goodbye.

Heart-Centered ♡ Approach Story

I could write a book solely on recruitment and onboarding stories. It's so fun. Nothing surprises me anymore. I'm sure you have some good tales too. My favorite background-check story is when I was recruiting for a client. The first candidate to whom we made an offer had a clear background screening. However, in doing a Google search, something derogatory was found. The client wanted to rescind the offer. The candidate was devastated.

The second candidate to whom we made an offer had a criminal history in their background screening. The client wanted to overlook it. I asked the client if they were interested in a legal claim against them if they provided an opportunity to a candidate with a criminal history, and not the original candidate who did not. Of course the answer was no, and we continued the search.

The third time was the charm – and employee and employer are still happily ever after as of the writing of this book after more than two years!

Another shocker: An employee switched their first name and last name to pass the background screening, so the report came back clean even though the employee had a criminal record! It was six months before the error was realized. Very sneaky! Apparently, criminal information is only stored under name and date of birth. For example, if the name sent to the court is TEST NAME 10/20/1963, the researcher or clerk will say "no records found." The Social Security Number (SSN) trace just automatically validates if the SSN is valid, and then sends addresses associated with this person.

Retention and Turnover

Create a long-term commitment to value individuals for their unique contributions and holistic well-being.

This will minimize turnover and position organizations for long-term retention success.

Chapter 6

The Spin Cycle of Staffing: Retention and Turnover

Train people well enough so they can leave.
Treat them well enough, so they don't want to.

—RICHARD BRANSON, FOUNDER OF THE VIRGIN GROUP

When we look at an employee's lifecycle, we could say it mirrors the twirls and turns clothes go through in a washer and dryer, which is a bit like a dance. The wash represents recruitment and onboarding (Chapter 5). The rhythmic motion of washing clothes mirrors the challenges and growth encountered during employment. The rinse and spin phase is like the dynamics of retention and the potential for turnover. Just as the dance of a dryer concludes the cycle, employees emerge, like clean, dry clothes, revitalized and poised for new opportunities. *The Heart-Centered Approach* has a transformative effect on employees by using the best retention practices.

Branson is a perfect example of leading with the *Heart-Centered Approach*. He understands that *not* caring for his employees far outweighs the *potential* risk of an employee leaving. The first lesson: change your mindset. *Stop* thinking about when your new hire's last day might be, and instead, *start* thinking about their professional development, and valuing your employees as humans! The consequence, if not done, is watching a spin cycle of staffing. Make caring for your employees a *top* priority. Your employees will *always* be your greatest asset.

The Spin Cycle in an Employee's Lifecycle

Retention and turnover are intricately connected, each influencing the other in a continuous spin-cycle dance. In order to understand, we must first learn the steps of the dance in the shoes of the employees and consider their motivations and choices. Employees are humans with hearts, not machines with coils; they are complex beings with aspirations, needs, and a desire for growth. Their decisions to stay or leave are influenced by many factors, both personal and professional. Allow me to take the lead on this dance, and I welcome you to follow:

Continuous Movement: In both a spin cycle and an employee's lifecycle, there is a continuous movement. In the case of the spin cycle, clothes are constantly in motion, undergoing a process of cleaning and renewal. Similarly, employees are always in motion within their careers, experiencing growth, challenges, and changes, both personally and professionally.

Cycles of Change: Employees go through different phases in their personal and professional lives, from onboarding and skill development, to taking on new responsibilities and, eventually, considering other personal opportunities including remaining single, getting married, or having children.

Cleaning and Renewal: Organizations strive to nurture and retain talent, help them grow, and renew their commitment to the organization. Employees also have cycles of personal growth and self-improvement.

Retention vs. Turnover: The spin cycle aims to retain and refresh clothes, just as organizations aim to retain their employees. However, just as clothes may occasionally wear out or become damaged, employees may also decide to move on to new opportunities, representing turnover.

Optimization and Maintenance: To ensure a spin cycle is effective, the washing machine must be well-maintained, and the settings must be optimized for the best results. Similarly, organizations need to maintain a supportive work environment and optimize their human resource practices to retain talent effectively.

Balancing Factors: The spin cycle balances factors like water temperature, detergent, and cycle duration to achieve the desired outcome. Organizations must balance various factors like compensation, career growth, work-life integration, and a positive work culture to retain and engage employees.

Adjusting Speed: In some cases, the spin cycle may need to adjust its speed to avoid damaging delicate fabrics. Similarly, organizations may need to adapt their strategies to accommodate the uniqueness of employees with different needs to prevent turnover.

Feedback Loop: Modern washing machines often have sensors and feedback mechanisms to ensure the cycle is proceeding smoothly. Organizations can benefit from feedback mechanisms like employee surveys, and stay and exit interviews to gather insights and make improvements in retention strategies.

Although the comparison of an employee's lifecycle to a spin cycle may have brought a few giggles, understand that both involve cycles, maintenance, and the need for adjustments to achieve the best outcomes. By understanding these dynamics, organizations can better navigate the challenges of retention and turnover.

Why Employees Leave Within a Year

One example of why employees leave within a year is a lack of career development, which shows the importance of creating purpose! It is only human for an individual to want to learn, grow, and take on new challenges. But this is not the issue – the issue is leaders are not accepting this. There are several understandable reasons:

- Loss of talent can be a significant blow to a team or an organization
- Investment and time are lost
- Concern about the impact on team dynamics, especially if a key collaborator
- Disruption in the succession plan
- Worry about losing valuable insights, knowledge, or clients to a competing organization

By nurturing a culture that encourages learning and growth, leaders can increase the likelihood of retaining their top talent. *Show* you care so they never want to say goodbye, and spend the money on the front end for training and development because it will pay off in the long run! **There are policies an organization can put in place so money is not lost should an employee leave within a year of training and development.**

Another example employees may leave is because of compensation. If employees feel they are underpaid or the benefit package is not competitive, they may explore other options. However, the solution is not always a higher-paying job – it's financial wellness. Surprised? Don't be. A majority of employees live paycheck to paycheck, regardless of income. It isn't about making more money as much as it is about educating employees on how to manage their money wisely. By lowering the financial stress level and helping employees manage their finances, the chances of retention are much greater. Why? You are showing you care and leading with the *Heart-Centered Approach.* Is there a cost to financial wellness programs? Yes, but the costs will vary depending on the size of your organization and the scope. However, again, you will be spending much less than what it will take to replace an employee.

Examples of financial wellness programs to provide:

- Workshops on budgeting, saving, investing, and retirement planning
- Resources and guidance on managing and reducing debt, tax planning, and savings programs

- One-on-one financial counseling sessions with certified financial planners or advisors
- Flexible Spending Accounts (FSAs) and Health Savings Accounts (HSAs)
- Employee Assistance Programs (EAPs)

A third factor that may cause employees to leave in their first year is a *bad* manager! Employees don't leave companies, they leave managers. I see it all the time when reviewing a candidate's resume. I ask, why did you leave Company ABC? Candidates respond, "change in management." Say no more. When an employee feels underappreciated, micromanaged, lack of trust and communication, or unempowered, they say good-bye. If an organization wants to reduce turnover rates, they must train their managers to:

- Set expectations and have clear guidelines
- Keep communication open for questions, comments, and collaboration, including listening and providing constructive feedback regularly, not just annually
- Empower their teams to make decisions
- Delegate and walk away, providing employees full ownership and holding them accountable

Other spin-cycle setting reasons for turnover and solutions for retention are:

Work-Life Integration: Excessive workload, long hours, and an inability to manage work and personal life. *Solution: Show you value their time by ensuring they take lunch breaks, paid time off to* *avoid burnout, set clear boundaries for after-hours communication, and have a flexible work arrangement.*

Organizational Culture: An unhealthy or toxic work environment. *Solution: A positive, inclusive, and respectful culture is vital for retention.*

Lack of Recognition: Feeling undervalued or unappreciated. *Solution: Publicly praise and implement recognition and appreciation programs that acknowledge employees' contributions.*

Conflict with Co-workers: Interpersonal conflicts with colleagues or team members can make the workplace uncomfortable. *Solution: Develop training for conflict resolution and address conflicts promptly and impartially.*

Organizational Changes: Major shifts within the organization, such as restructuring, layoffs, or mergers. *Solution: Transparent communication is key during periods of change. Provide support, resources, and training to help employees adapt to new structures or processes.*

Geographic Relocation or Health Reasons: Life Happens! These situations are out of anyone's control. *Solution: Accommodate with remote work options if their job role may accommodate them. The key is communication and leading with the Heart-Centered Approach.*

The True Cost Factors of Turnover

For those of you who like numbers, let me spell out the cost with the following example: An employee makes $60,000 a year, the organization invests five percent (5%) annually into training and development, and the employee leaves after one (1) year because the organization was not flexible with an employee's hours to accommodate their child's new bus schedule.

Heart-Centered Approach: $60,000 X 0.05 = **$3,000** annual cost to the organization

Lack of Heart: $60,000 ÷ 12 months = $5,000/month X 6 months (average cost of an employee's salary to replace them) = **$30,000**

Heart-Centered Approach? Or Lack of Heart? Which would you prefer to pay? The average cost to replace an employee is six (6) months' salary – *this is not a typo*. Without proper recruitment and onboarding practices in place, as discussed in Chapter 5, and making your employees a top priority, the consequence will be watching a spin cycle of staffing and new hires leave within the first year of employment.

Additional costs of spin-cycle turnover have a multitude of factors, and the size of the organization may impact the magnitude of these cost factors. Cost examples related to the $30,000 example above:

Recruitment Costs: These include expenses related to job postings, advertising, and recruitment agency fees. The process of sourcing, screening, and interviewing candidates can be time-consuming and costly. Beyond recruitment expenses, there are costs associated with conducting background checks, drug screenings, or fingerprinting.

Onboarding Costs: Properly onboarding a new employee involves training, orientation, and administrative tasks. These expenditures can accumulate, particularly if there's a steep learning curve for the role.

Productivity Loss: When an employee leaves, there's often a temporary loss of productivity as the organization searches for a replacement, and the team adjusts to the absence. Overtime or temporary staffing costs may also be incurred to fill the gap.

Training and Development: If the departing employee received significant training and development, these costs could be considered a loss when they leave. An organization may need to invest in similar training for the replacement. In addition, new employees typically require time to become fully productive. During this transition period, existing employees may spend additional time training and mentoring the new hire, diverting their focus from other tasks.

Legal Costs and Benefits: In some cases, turnover may result in legal costs, such as: severance negotiations or pay; disputes over non-compete agreements; or other legal proceedings; as well as paying for continued benefits or accrued time off to departing employees.

Customer Impact: Employee turnover can impact customer relationships, particularly if the departing employee had key client contacts. Losing clients due to the departure can have significant financial repercussions.

Knowledge Drain: Departing employees take institutional knowledge with them, which can lead to inefficiencies, errors, and lost opportunities. The time and resources required to rebuild that knowledge within the organization are often underestimated.

Cultural Impact: High turnover can erode an organization's culture and employee morale, leading to decreased engagement and potentially more turnover in a cascading effect.

The true cost factors associated with turnover are a compelling reminder of the importance of proactive retention efforts.

A Generational Issue?

The answer is no. The challenges on retention and turnover should not be considered a generational issue. Gallup is a company that conducts many different surveys to help organizations understand workforce engagement and the influence of a positive workplace. One of their studies showed that employee engagement was very similar across the board. See the chart below from my friend, David Miklas, Esq., an employment law attorney in Florida.

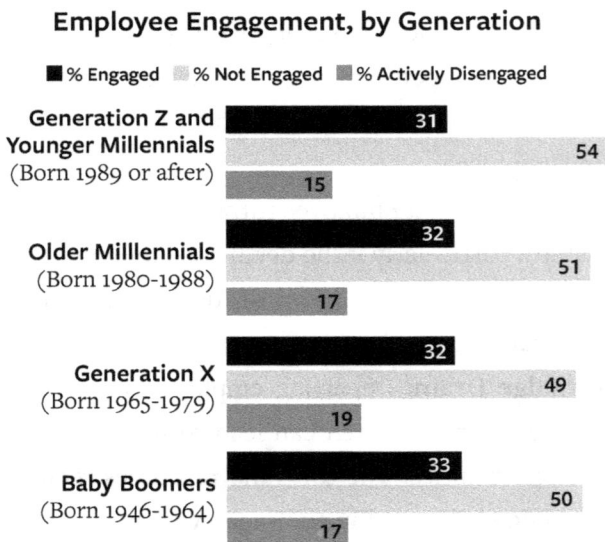

Employee Engagement, by Generation

■ % Engaged ▨ % Not Engaged ■ % Actively Disengaged

Generation Z and Younger Millennials (Born 1989 or after)	31 / 54 / 15
Older Milllennials (Born 1980-1988)	32 / 51 / 17
Generation X (Born 1965-1979)	32 / 49 / 19
Baby Boomers (Born 1946-1964)	33 / 50 / 17

The generational differences in the workplace stereotypes or judges employees based on their generation. Instead, foster an inclusive culture, train leaders to communicate with the *Heart-Centered Approach*, and be clear on expectations no matter the generation. Leaders need to understand their workforce: their wants, interests, and needs ("WINs") – and it has nothing to do with the employees' generation.

The Heart-Centered Approach Path Forward

As organizations navigate the spin-cycle between retention and turnover, they must recognize that the *Heart-Centered Approach* is not a quick fix, but a long-term commitment to create a workplace that values individuals for their unique contributions and holistic well-being. In doing so, organizations can achieve lasting success in the ever-evolving, spin-cycle of staffing. High-performing organizations view retention as a strategic imperative, recognizing that it goes beyond compensation and benefits. Organizations that invest in their employees are not only better equipped to minimize turnover spin cycles, but also positioned for long-term retention success.

♡ HEART TAKEAWAY

Both spin cycles and an employee's life cycle involve the need to cleanse and refresh periodically so individuals can engage in practices and rituals to keep themselves mentally and emotionally renewed and ready to face life's challenges, personally and professionally.

Heart-Centered ♡ Approach Story

When the world shut down on March 17, 2020, and we began to isolate and live in a ZOOM world due to the COVID-19 Pandemic, this Human Optimizer's spin cycle felt like it was stuck. Like many of you, I had plenty of time to reflect on my purpose, life, and career. You see, five weeks after the world shut down, my mother died of metastatic breast cancer in Cleveland, Ohio – alone – and I had to ZOOM her funeral from Florida. And because no one knew how to work ZOOM yet, it shut down after 30 minutes.

Four months later, my daughter, Lauren, was visiting me on vacation. At the time, I had worked for this company for a year and a half, and I was due for my mid-year review – over ZOOM. While I was receiving my review, I pampered Lauren with a $160 specialty curly haircut at the hair salon next to my office. I opened up my ZOOM link full of confidence, anticipation, and excitement as I was getting to hang with Lauren after my review – and there was my boss standing in a *Superhero Pose*. As I commented on the stance, my boss said, "Karen, we are not giving you a mid-year review today; we are terminating your position."

Yes, yes, yes – you are probably as confused as I was; but my oldest brother, David, always has great wisdom, some of which I should have listened to better. David taught me that when there is nothing left to say, simply say, "Thank You." So I did, and added, "Thank you for the opportunity." I left the ZOOM room, went to the beach with Lauren, and my boss was kind enough to allow me to come back after hours to clean out my office.

So, while my career as I knew it ended via ZOOM may sound devastating, and admittedly I was a little panicked that I had to pay for that $160 curly haircut (I mean, can we put the hair back on now?), the push out the window provided an opportunity for me to move forward with my own company, HR by Karen, LLC, which I created a month earlier.

Three days after my termination, I attended the 2020 HR Florida Annual Conference in Orlando, Florida. Ellen Latham, MS, Owner of Orangetheory Fitness, was our last Keynote Speaker. While I discussed my transition with my fellow HR colleagues and dear friends Jessica Holloman and Rich Williams, who encouraged me to take the risk, it was Ellen who inspired me. She allowed me to throw fear out of my mindset and gave me the confidence to go *crush it!* During her one-hour keynote Ellen was a model for me:

1. At 55 years old (*which I was at the time*),
2. In an industry (*fitness*) she had been in for 30 years (*I had been in the legal industry for 30 years*),
3. As a single mom (*check*),
4. With a small wallet (*triple check*),
5. Her position was eliminated (mic drop)!

As the attendees were sitting six feet apart from one another, after each of these points were made, Jessica turned and asked, "*Did you hear that...*" As tears streamed down my face, I heard the message loud and clear. As I drove home from the conference, I knew I finally found my purpose. I asked myself the same questions Ellen asked herself: *Why not me? Why not follow my dreams?*

Why can't I be successful? I wrote these three words, "Why Not Me," on a Post-It note and stuck it on my mirror in my bathroom so I would see it every single day, and...it is still there. My business color is orange as a reminder of who inspired me.

Sometimes, when we get stuck in the spin cycle, it is up to us as leaders to get unstuck and navigate obstacles, and turn them into opportunities. Life does not happen *to* us – it happens *for* us. It is up to us as leaders to *make* things happen. Charles Swindoll said, "Life is 10% what happens to you, and 90% how you react to it." The obstacles are always going to come; it is our choice how we react. When you lead with the *Heart-Centered Approach*, there is no obstacle you won't be able to overcome.

The *best* thing that ever happened to me was being terminated via ZOOM. I now share my story with leaders everywhere – presenting keynotes on topics such as leadership, self-awareness, and the importance of a positive, growth mindset. I especially love to share how to properly stand in a *superhero pose* – because when standing in a *superhero pose*, we feel more confident, empowered, and energized. Our bodies change our minds, and our minds change our behavior, and our behavior changes our outcomes!

Change Management

Embrace change and be willing to evolve and adapt.

This will allow organizations to stay relevant and competitive.

Chapter 7

Dancing Through the Rhythms of Transformation

Change your opinions, keep to your principles;
change your leaves, keep intact your roots.

—VICTOR HUGO, POET AND NOVELIST

Let's keep our rhythm as we dance through the transformation of change management. As you and your organization navigate the rhythms of change, remember Victor Hugo's wisdom. Organizations can change and adapt their strategies, structures, and processes as needed; but they should do so while holding true to their core principles, values, and identity. Keep your core principles, even as you change your procedures. This balance enables your organizations to evolve and flourish in a dynamic business environment while maintaining your roots and authenticity.

In the world of organizations, change is often driven by external factors such as market trends, technological advancements, or shifts in customer preferences. To thrive, organizations must be adaptable and open to a change in their opinions or strategies when necessary. However, while opinions and strategies may need to evolve, the core principles and values of an organization should remain steadfast. These principles are the beliefs that define the organization's identity, culture, and ethical standards. They provide a moral compass that guides decision-making, even in times of change.

The metaphorical dance of organizational change represents the ability to adapt, shift, or change certain aspects of a dance routine (opinions) while staying grounded and true to the fundamental core of the dance (principles). A dancer pivots along the dance floor maintaining one foot in place (the root) while the other foot sweeps and changes direction (the leaves). An organization's products, services, processes, and even its branding may change and evolve over time; however, the organization's core identity, values, and culture should always remain constant, providing stability and retaining its fundamental essence.

The Dance of Transformation: A *Heart-Centered Approach* Perspective

In the *Heart-Centered Approach* to change management, the *Dance of Transformation* embodies the organization's journey of evolving, adapting, and growing while nurturing the well-being and emotions of its employees and stakeholders (external consultants or experts, customers and clients, suppliers and partners, or advisory boards). Each stakeholder contributes to the successful navigation of the dance of transformation, making it a more harmonious and purpose-driven journey.

Here's what the dance looks like:

Align with Values and Purpose: The dance begins with a deep reflection on the organization's core values and purpose. Just as a dance has a rhythm and melody, organizations must align their actions with a harmonious blend of their values and purpose. This alignment serves as the guiding music that sets the tone for the entire transformation journey.

Listen with Empathy: In the dance of transformation, leaders take the role of attentive partners. They listen actively to the concerns, aspirations, and feedback of employees and stakeholders. This empathetic connection forms the foundation of trust and understanding, much like two dancers in sync with each other's movements.

Communicate as a Dance Step: Effective communication is a pivotal step in the dance. Communication is not a monologue, but a dialogue that invites engagement from all participants. Messages are conveyed with clarity, authenticity, and sensitivity, ensuring that everyone is on the same page and knows their role in the dance.

Navigate Change Rhythms: Change is dynamic and rhythmic, like various dance styles. Sometimes, it is a waltz, steady and graceful; other times, it is a tango, passionate and intense. Organizations must adapt to the changing rhythms of transformation. The *Heart-Centered Approach* encourages leaders to recognize when to lead with assertiveness and when to yield to the flow of change.

Care for Emotional Well-Being: Emotional well-being is at the heart of this dance. Leaders and organizations must acknowledge and address the emotional responses that change can evoke. Just as dance partners support each other's balance and comfort, organizations provide resources, counseling, and a supportive environment to help employees navigate emotional challenges.

Include and Collaborate: The dance of transformation is inclusive. Everyone is invited to participate, regardless of their role or position. Collaborative movements ensure that diverse perspectives and talents contribute to the choreography of change. Inclusivity is not only about inviting others, but also valuing their unique contributions.

Ethical Leadership and Integrity: Ethical leadership is a constant presence in the dance. Leaders must maintain their integrity and uphold the organization's ethical principles. Ethical conduct is non-negotiable, ensuring that the dance remains authentic and respectful of individuals and stakeholders.

Learn and Adapt: Just as dancers refine their movements with practice, organizations embrace a culture of continuous learning. The dance of transformation encourages adaptation, experimentation, and the willingness to learn from missteps and make it part of the dance. It's an acknowledgment that perfection is not the goal – growth is.

Celebrate Milestones and Achievements: As in any dance, celebrating milestones is essential. Organizations mark achievements along the transformation journey, acknowledging the hard work, resilience, and dedication of everyone involved. Celebration strengthens the sense of unity and accomplishment.

Sustain the Rhythm Over Time: The dance of transformation is not a one-time performance but a continuous rhythm. Organizations aim to sustain the momentum, ensuring that the rhythm of change becomes an intrinsic part of their culture. It's about embedding the *Heart-Centered Approach* into the organization's DNA.

The *Dance of Transformation* within the *Heart-Centered Approach* is a dynamic, inclusive, and empathetic journey. It's a dance where leaders and employees move together, adapting to changing rhythms while honoring values, emotions, and ethical principles. This dance is a powerful metaphor for change management that prioritizes the well-being of individuals and ensures that the transformation journey is both effective and human-centered.

Common Challenges in the Dance of Transformation

Just as dancers face obstacles on the dance floor, organizations may encounter hurdles when embracing change. Let's explore the top 10 complexities and uncertainties that often arise during change initiatives, how these challenges can impact the organization as a whole and the stakeholders, and how to overcome each challenge.

1. **Resistance to Change – The Unexpected Dance Partner:** Just as in a dance, there can be unexpected resistance. Resistance to change often emerges when individuals feel their routines disrupted. *Solution: Encourage open dialogue, listen empathetically to concerns, and involve employees in the change process. Demonstrate the benefits of change and provide training and support to help individuals adapt to new routines.*

2. **Uncertainty and Anxiety – The Tempo Changes:** The unpredictable tempo can lead to uncertainty and anxiety among employees. *Solution: Maintain clear and transparent communication throughout the change journey. Provide regular updates to address anxieties, explain the rationale behind changes, and offer emotional support and resources for coping.*

3. **Lack of Alignment – Out of Step:** Sometimes, employees may feel out of step when change initiatives don't align with their core beliefs. *Solution: Prioritize alignment between the organization's values and change initiatives. Ensure that changes resonate with the Heart-Centered Approach's principles, and communicate the alignment clearly to employees to build trust.*

4. **Change Fatigue – Sustaining the Dance Energy:** Just as dancers can tire during a lengthy performance, employees may experience change fatigue if transformations are too frequent or too intense. *Solution: Pace change initiatives thoughtfully to prevent burnout. Implement well-being initiatives, recognize employees' efforts, and celebrate milestones to sustain motivation and energy levels.*

5. **Lack of Vision – Dancing Blindfolded:** Attempting the dance of transformation without a clear vision can lead to confusion and missteps. *Solution: Develop a clear and compelling vision for*

the change. Communicate the vision effectively to provide direction and purpose for the change journey, ensuring that everyone knows the steps and their role.

6. **Overlooking Employee Well-Being – Dance Injuries and Burnout:** In the rush of change, employee well-being can be overlooked, leading to burnout and emotional strain. *Solution: Prioritize emotional support to prevent injuries on the dance floor. Offer resources such as counseling and stress management programs. Create a supportive environment that allows employees to share their feelings and concerns openly.*

7. **Ineffective Communication – Misheard Steps:** Just as mis-communication can lead to missteps in a dance, ineffective communication during change initiatives can hinder progress. *Solution: Establish authentic, two-way communication channels to ensure everyone is in sync. Ensure that messages are clear, consistent, and tailored to the audience. Encourage feedback and active listening to prevent misunderstandings.*

8. **Lack of Inclusivity – A Solo Performance:** The *Heart-Centered Approach* advocates for inclusivity and collaboration, but sometimes change efforts may exclude certain groups. *Solution: Embrace inclusivity and collaboration to create a harmonious ensemble. Involve employees from diverse backgrounds and roles in change initiatives. Value their contributions, fostering a sense of belonging and shared ownership.*

9. **Sustainability Challenges – The Dance Must Go On:** Sustaining the momentum of change over time can be challenging. *Solution: Maintain a long-term commitment to change to ensure that change remains an integral part of the organization's culture. Embed*

change into the organization's culture, reinforcing its importance and revisiting and refreshing change initiatives regularly to keep the momentum alive.

10. **External Pressures – Adapting to New Dance Styles:** External factors, much like new dance styles, can force organizations to adapt rapidly. *Solution: Balance external pressures with internal values. Stay true to the Heart-Centered Approach's principles while remaining agile and adaptable to external changes. Continuously assess the impact of external factors on the dance of transformation.*

By addressing these common challenges and implementing the solutions within the *Heart-Centered Approach*, organizations can navigate the dance of transformation with grace and resilience. Ensure that change is not just a series of steps, but a heartfelt and purposeful journey toward growth and innovation. This helps organizations stay aligned with their values and maintain the well-being of their employees and stakeholders.

♡ HEART TAKEAWAY

Change is inevitable, and organizations that resist it can become stagnant or obsolete. Therefore, embracing change means a willingness to evolve and adapt, which allows organizations to stay relevant and competitive. While strategies and practices may change, maintaining cultural continuity is essential. It ensures that employees remain aligned with the organization's values and principles while at the same time fostering a sense of belonging and purpose. Organizations may change their strategies when they rebrand, enter new markets, or adopt new technologies. However, these changes should align with the organization's roots, its fundamental mission, and the principles that guide its actions. Next, we will continue our rhythm with more adventures as we gracefully dance through conflict resolution in Chapter 8.

Heart-Centered ♡ Approach Stories

In 2011, I was invited to a Thirty-One Gifts party. Thirty-One Gifts is one of the largest direct-selling companies in North America selling purses, totes, bags, and organizational gifts. This faith-based company was founded with the simple mission to empower and support women. I loved everything Cindy Monroe, founder of Thirty-One Gifts, stood for, and I joined Nicole Tutko's team and became a Bag Lady. Nicole led with love and showed me the path to success as a team leader with Thirty-One Gifts.

Cindy founded Thirty-One Gifts in the basement of her Chattanooga, Tennessee, home in 2003. In 2014, Thirty-One Gifts was named the fastest-growing woman-owned company worldwide, and now for over 20 years Cindy has helped support women and our families. I was a single mom looking for a second income and a purpose. Cindy gave me both. Three weeks after I joined as a consultant, the company made the tough decision to implement a recruiting freeze until July 2011. *Big* change! Although at first the change was scary because I could not build my team right away, just three months after the unfreeze, I became a director with Thirty-One Gifts. My team name was Shepherd's Stylin' Shells – and my leadership journey began.

Cindy leads with love and faith and is the epitome of the *Heart-Centered Approach*. I will forever be grateful for all the women I met through this company and what it provided for my daughter Lauren and I. God Bless you, Cindy Monroe. Thank you for believing in me.

Cindy Monroe's Story

Sometimes too much of a good thing can be... well, too much of a good thing. Seven years in, the company I founded in my basement in Chattanooga, Tennessee, in 2003 was suddenly experiencing exponential growth (okay, let's be real... *runaway growth!*). Since our launch, Thirty-One Gifts had seen steady year-over-year increases, but by the end of 2010, the company was exploding, with literally thousands of new consultants joining each month. *More* consultants meant *more* people connecting with *more* customers, all of whom wanted *more* of Thirty-One's bags, totes, and home products.

Sounds like heaven for a CEO, right? Not so much.

Our customer service call center couldn't keep up. Our operations team was falling behind. New manufacturing partners were struggling to maintain quality. So, we initiated massive hiring in just about every department. And while the additional staffing provided critical help, their inevitable inexperience led to things like orders going out the door with missing items. We had to admit to ourselves: We were chasing the ball down the hill, and the ball was winning. We needed to catch our breath before causing damage to our reputation. As an executive team, we made the difficult decision to put a six-month freeze on recruiting for new consultants. The pause allowed prospects to join a waitlist while we focused on getting our teams up to speed.

Perhaps my biggest takeaway as a CEO leading a company through this level of change was the absolute necessity of *communication, communication, communication.* We were up-front with the consultants, owning our missteps and being transparent about the need to put a hold on growth while we ramped up our ability to support that growth.

We also reached out to customers, apologizing for delays and mistakes, asking them to be patient with us while we made improvements to better serve them. And we made sure to recognize the hard work of our consultants in connecting with their customers and staying in touch with those on the waitlist. It was truly an all-hands-on-deck time for our Thirty-One family across the country, and I can't be more grateful to our consultants and customers who gave us grace and joined us in navigating the growth.

It certainly wasn't the first season of change for Thirty-One – or our last. Through each of them we have returned to our twelve values time and again – words and behaviors that reflect our culture, faith, integrity, and our commitment to empowering others. We not only communicate these values, but also we check ourselves, making adjustments as needed to live up to our mission.

We also feel it's important to celebrate the small wins and have fun, no matter the victories or challenges we're currently facing. At the Home Office, for example, there have been winter days when an announcement over the warehouse PA system has invited everyone outside for a snowman-building contest. We've brought in ping-pong tables for lunch-break tournaments in our operations area, and we've hosted chili cookoffs, philanthropic golf tournaments, paper airplane and pumpkin-carving contests, and so much more.

As a CEO now for 20 years, I can definitely attest that every company *will* encounter change, but the more you involve your team, listen to feedback, lean into your values, and communicate at every turn, the more you can experience success (and even joy!) along the way.

Conflict Resolution

Accept that conflict is unavoidable, and understand it is our actions, reactions, and perspectives that make conflict an opportunity for critical conversation.

This allows leaders opportunities to expand their emotional intelligence, communication skills, empathy, foster resilience and personal growth.

Chapter 8

The Adventure of Conflict Resolution

*For good ideas and true innovation, you need
human interaction, conflict, argument, and debate.*

—MARGARET HEFFERNAN, CEO AND AUTHOR

Most people instinctively avoid conflict, but a good disagreement is central to progress. Great teams, relationships, and businesses allow people to disagree. Conflict provides an opportunity for leaders, teams, and employees to grow personally and professionally. Just as adventurers find hidden treasures during their journeys, when conflict resolution is approached with a heart-centered mindset, it can strengthen relationships rather than damage them.

In conflict, there are two things to remember: 1) it is unavoidable, and 2) how we resolve it is in our control. Our actions and reactions will make a conflict either an opportunity or a critical conversation. Similar to adventures, conflict resolution often involves navigating uncharted territories. Conflicts can be complex, with unexpected twists and turns. Approaching conflict resolution as an adventure means exploring new perspectives, understanding underlying issues, and implementing innovative solutions. Conflict resolution challenges everyone to overcome obstacles and allows individuals the opportunity to expand their emotional intelligence, hone communication skills, and foster resilience.

The Emotional Journey with Conflict Resolution

To successfully navigate conflicts, we need to understand how we operate and process, and what makes us human. Like it or not, we all feel emotion! Our perceptions lead to emotions, which then lead to our actions. The basic, core emotions that influence our human behavior are: happiness, sadness, trust, fear, anger, joy, anticipation, and surprise. For leaders to understand how to handle difficult situations they must know how to manage emotions. Oftentimes, an individual's emotion is misunderstood. There are multiple factors that can lead to misunderstandings:

Non-Verbal Communication is the unspoken language of body movements, facial expressions, and tone of voice, which may significantly impact emotional exchanges. Misinterpretations of these cues may lead to conflicts, emphasizing the importance of clarity and awareness in non-verbal communication. **Solution***: Foster open communication, encouraging employees to express themselves explicitly, and providing forums for discussions to clarify intentions will reduce the chances of conflict.*

Lack of Empathy is not making an effort to understand the emotions of others. Failure to empathize with others' emotions can create distance and exacerbate conflicts. **Solution***: Establish practices that encourage individuals to consider others' perspectives using active listening that fosters a supportive environment, minimizing misunderstandings and conflicts.*

Assumptions, Biases, and Stereotypes are preconceived notions that may cloud our perception, contributing to conflicts. **Solution***: Address preconceived notions with ongoing education that increases self-awareness, and implement diversity and inclusion training that will foster a mindset of curiosity, contributing to a more equitable and conflict-resistant workplace.*

Cultural Differences are diverse backgrounds, varying norms, and expectations. These differences may potentially lead to clashes in the workplace. **Solution:** *Embrace cultural sensitivity and encourage open dialogue that helps bridge these gaps, encouraging a more inclusive and harmonious atmosphere.*

Individual Variation is recognizing and respecting the uniqueness of each individual. Failing to understand that people have different stories and experiences may create conflicts rooted in personal differences. **Solution:** *Create an inclusive culture that values diversity and encourages employees to appreciate each other's unique strengths and perspectives – which will contribute to a peaceful work environment.*

Hidden Emotions are unexpressed feelings and an unwillingness to be transparent and honest. This may create tension and complications in the workplace. **Solution:** *Encourage transparent communication and provide a safe space for individuals to* *share their emotions that will help uncover hidden issues and prevent conflicts from escalating.*

Generally, when there are misunderstandings in communicating with others, there is a lack of clarity because one or more of the above factors play a significant role in conveying emotions, leading to misinterpretations. Leaders must understand the complexity of emotions. They are dynamic and can change rapidly. What an individual feels at one moment may shift in response to changing circumstances. Individuals' feelings can change *on a dime* in response to a wide range of circumstances and triggers.

For example, a person who initially feels excited about a new job opportunity may experience a shift in emotions to anxiety when they realize the increased responsibility that comes with the role. Similarly, someone feeling content during a leisurely walk in a park may become irritable if it suddenly starts raining. The triggers for these emotional shifts can be diverse, including external events, other individuals, or internal thoughts. A disappointing news article may trigger feelings of sadness or anger, while a kind gesture from a friend can evoke feelings of happiness. Moreover, the state of physical well-being, such as hunger, fatigue, or illness, can influence emotions. These examples illustrate the dynamic nature of emotions and how they respond to the ever-changing circumstances, and internal and external factors that individuals encounter in their daily lives.

Another emotional disrupter is the confusion between an individual feeling passionate versus emotional. Feeling passionate can sometimes be mistaken for reacting emotionally due to the intensity of both expressions, but it is important to note that the two are distinct concepts. Emotions are temporary and immediate feelings influenced by various stimuli, events, or situations. Whereas, passion is more of a commitment or dedication – our driving force in what motivates us on a particular activity, cause, group, or person. An observer not aware of an individual's underlying motivation or the context of their expression may misinterpret passion as emotional intensity.

For example, someone who speaks passionately about their work or a cause may be perceived as overly emotional, which may not be the issue at all, as their intensity is rooted in dedication and commitment. Physical expressions of passion, such as hand gestures or an animated tone, may also resemble those used when experiencing strong emotions. However, without understanding the context, and keeping in mind the factors discussed above, individuals may not differentiate between passion and emotions, which can lead to misplaced concern or criticism. The best way to avoid this confusion is to clearly communicate to help others understand the source of their emotion, as our emotions are a *huge* part of the *human* experience and interaction.

Using Assessments as a Tool

Assessment tools play a crucial role in understanding individual and team dynamics within an organization, offering insights into personality traits, communication styles, and strengths. Here's an overview of several widely used assessments, and their potential positive impact on Return on Investment (ROI), which I have experienced:

DISC Assessment

Purpose: DISC assesses behavioral styles, categorizing individuals into Dominance, Influence, Steadiness, and Conscientiousness.	**ROI Impact:** Understanding team dynamics and communication styles can enhance collaboration and minimize conflicts, leading to improved productivity and efficiency.

Myers-Briggs Type Indicator (MBTI)

Purpose: MBTI categorizes individuals into personality types based on preferences in four dichotomies (Extraversion/Introversion, Sensing/Intuition, Thinking/Feeling, Judging/Perceiving).	**ROI Impact:** When diverse thinking patterns are recognized, organizations can optimize team structures, foster effective communication, and tailor leadership approaches. This results in improved teamwork and employee satisfaction.

Gallup Clifton Strengths Analysis:

Purpose: Identifies individuals' top strengths out of 34 themes, providing insights into natural talents.	**ROI Impact:** Aligning roles with employees' strengths enhances job satisfaction, productivity, and engagement. Leveraging a variety of strengths builds high-performing teams.

Predictive Index (PI):	
Purpose: PI evaluates workplace behaviors, focusing on factors like dominance, extroversion, patience, and formality.	**ROI Impact:** Aligning roles with individuals' natural behaviors helps optimize talent. This leads to improved job performance, employee engagement, and reduced turnover.

TraitSet:	
Purpose: Measures traits around leadership and management, evaluating personality traits and behavioral tendencies, such as a good work ethic and integrity.	**ROI Impact:** Provides a comprehensive view of individual characteristics, aiding in effective leadership development, team building, and talent management, which ultimately contributes to organizational success.

Overall, by incorporating assessment tools into conflict resolution processes, organizations can create a more nuanced and tailored approach, ultimately leading to more effective and sustainable solutions. These tools empower individuals and teams to navigate conflicts with a deeper understanding of themselves and their colleagues, fostering a positive and constructive workplace culture.

Reflect to Understand

As leaders, in order to facilitate constructive resolution, we need to gain insight. This self-awareness is an integral part of the *Heart-Centered Approach* to conflict resolution. So, let's go on an adventure. Think about a recent conflict you had. Do you have it? Ask yourself these questions:

What were your emotions during the conflict, and how intense were they? If we understand our emotional responses, we are able to manage them more effectively.

What were the triggers or events that led to the disagreement or tension? Recognizing the root causes can help address underlying issues.

What words, actions, or behaviors did you have to contribute to the situation? This may be hard for some of you to answer because of that "A" word... *Accountability*. Taking responsibility for your part is essential for conflict resolution.

What were their perspectives, or what were they experiencing during the conflict? We don't always know what someone's story is or what chapter they are in. Therefore, it is important to empathize with others' viewpoints and understand their needs.

What were the communication breakdowns? Were there misunderstandings, misinterpretations, or ineffective communication patterns? Identifying communication challenges can guide improvements.

What were the core issues at the heart of the conflict? Pinpointing these fundamental needs, values, or goals is vital for finding common ground.

You are doing great! I encourage you to dive deeper into your reflection. Don't be afraid. This is making you stronger and braver. Move into your superhero power pose if you need to, as you will need this confidence in the next step!

What were you trying to achieve – your goals and objectives? Assess whether your goals were aligned with a productive resolution or if they escalated the conflict.

What could you have done differently to have led to a more positive outcome? Remember, we are on an adventure, so explore the alternative approaches and behaviors that could have been employed during the conflict. Identifying these possibilities promotes personal growth.

What were the lessons learned that can be applied to future situations? Not all conflict is bad. Conflict can be a valuable source of learning.

What steps can you take to mend any emotional wound and move forward constructively? It is time to set your ego aside, not take it personally, and consider the strategies for repairing and rebuilding the relationship... if you choose to do so. However, recognize that there is always a consequence to our choices.

What proactive measures can you take? For example, implement training on improved communication or, the obvious, conflict resolution! Think about ways to prevent similar conflicts in the future.

From what individuals or resources can I seek guidance? Guidance can come from your friendly HR professional, a colleague, or a mentor. Seeking out guidance and asking for support to resolve the conflict can be very beneficial.

Finally, outline the next steps for addressing the conflict and the actions you will take to initiate the resolution or prevent a recurrence. Making a plan is essential! By asking these reflective questions, you will gain a deeper understanding of conflicts, your contributions, and your opportunities for constructive resolution.

Engagement

Now that you have clarity on yourself, your emotions, and your process, the next step in the adventure of conflict resolution is *engagement*. Conflict resolution is not solely about finding a solution, but also about strengthening relationships, fostering a culture of understanding and collaboration within the organization, and nurturing human connections. Addressing conflicts promptly and effectively will be less disruptive and detrimental to the organization, as the cost of unresolved conflict is immense, and a major source of stress, burnout, harassment, and sabotage. Train your leaders how to deal with conflict effectively with the *Heart-Centered Approach* in order to receive a positive outcome and follow the *10 Steps of Engagement* below:

Step 1: Initiate the Conversation: This first step sets the tone for the entire interaction and lays the foundation for constructive engagement. Timing and environment matter. Select a suitable time and a private, neutral space for the conversation, minimizing distractions and interruptions. This ensures that everyone can focus on the discussion without feeling rushed or exposed. Start the conversation by expressing your intentions clearly and honestly. Communicate your desire to resolve the conflict, emphasizing that the goal is not to assign blame but to find common ground and reach a solution together.

Step 2: Active Listening: This is more than just a passive act of hearing; it is an active and engaged process that demonstrates your commitment to understanding and empathizing with others. *Be present!* Put aside distractions like your smartphones or internal thoughts that may hinder your focus. Keep in mind – your body language communicates as much as your words. Maintain eye contact, face the individual, and use open and inviting gestures like nodding or leaning forward to show your engagement. Try to understand their perspective, emotions, and needs. Put yourself in their shoes to fully grasp their point of view. Empathize with their feelings, even if you don't agree with them. *Please* resist the urge to interrupt or offer solutions prematurely. Let the other person express themself fully before you respond. Interrupting can disrupt the flow and make them feel unheard. Show respect, be patient and comfortable with moments of silence, and avoid making judgments or forming opinions prematurely.

Step 3: Share Your Reflections: Share the insights gained during your self-reflection process. This includes acknowledging your own contributions (holding yourself accountable) to the conflict and expressing a sincere commitment to resolving it constructively. A good way to start is to acknowledge the other person's perspective and experiences by saying "I understand that you feel..." or "I can see how important this is to you..." and validate their emotions. This step will foster an environment of trust and mutual understanding.

Step 4: Clarify Misunderstandings: Use the 5 C's in Step 6 to clarify any misunderstandings or misinterpretations that may have contributed to the conflict. Ensure that everyone involved has a clear and accurate understanding of each other's perspectives. Be curious and ask questions. When encouraging an open dialogue, preconceived notions and assumptions can be corrected and clarified to pave the way for a sense of understanding and finding solutions between the parties.

Step 5: Seek Common Ground: Explore potential solutions or compromises that align with the needs and goals of all parties. When shared interests and values are identified, individuals can move beyond their differences and work together to find solutions that benefit everyone involved. Emphasize the "win-win" aspect of the resolution.

Step 6: Use Effective Communication: Effective communication is the compass that guides us through the twists and turns of challenging interpersonal terrain. John F. Kennedy said, *"The best way to resolve any conflict is through open and honest communication."* The 5 C's – clarity, curiosity, collaboration, compassion, and constructive engagement, serve as our steadfast companions on this journey.

- Clarity ensures that our messages are understood without ambiguity, paving the way for constructive dialogue.
- Curiosity propels us to seek a deeper understanding of the perspectives and emotions of those involved, fostering empathy and open-mindedness.
- Collaboration underscores the importance of working together to find solutions that benefit all parties, turning conflicts into opportunities for growth.

- Compassion reminds us to approach conflicts with understanding and kindness, preserving the delicate fabric of human connections.
- Constructive engagement drives us to transform disagreements into pathways for positive change, ensuring that our communication leads to resolution rather than escalation.

Caution: The only time this winning combination of effective communication may fail is if the other party has no accountability and has not self-reflected.

Step 7: Collaborative Problem-Solving: Work together to generate solutions and strategies for resolving the conflict. Encourage creative thinking and explore different approaches that address the core issues. Resolution is a joint effort that brings diverse perspectives to the table and that sparks creative and innovative solutions.

Step 8: Agreement and Commitment: This step solidifies the understanding and solutions reached during the conflict resolution process; outlines the specific actions, compromises, or changes to which all parties have consented; and defines the roles, responsibilities, and expectations of each party moving forward. The commitment ensures real actions using monitoring and accountability, and builds mutual trust and provides closure in order to move forward.

Step 9: Monitor and Follow-Up: Monitoring the situation is important to ensure that the agreed-upon actions are implemented, and that the conflict does not resurface. Regular follow-ups ensure that the resolution remains effective, sustainable, and adaptable to changing circumstances. Through ongoing communication, accountability, and evaluation, parties can transform conflict into a lasting positive outcome.

Step 10: Learn and Grow: View the conflict resolution process as an opportunity for personal and collective growth, self-discovery, recognizing the emotional hurdles, applying knowledge, identifying areas for improvement, building resilience, promoting positive change, celebrating progress, and embracing the adventure! Reflect on the experience and consider what lessons can be applied to future situations to prevent conflicts or address them more effectively.

Detours When Steps Fall Short

All organizations have conflict. That is inevitable when you bring people together with a wide diversity of personalities and backgrounds. Sometimes, the steps will fall short of finding a resolution. Therefore, take a detour on your adventure, reassess the situation, and consider alternative routes, such as:

Stay Calm and Patient: It's essential to remain composed and patient. Conflicts can be emotionally charged, and letting frustration or anger escalate can make matters worse. Sometimes, stepping away from the conflict temporarily can provide clarity and reduce tension.

Stay Neutral: Sometimes, it can be helpful to seek advice from a neutral party who is not directly involved in the conflict. They may offer a fresh perspective and potential solutions that the parties in conflict haven't considered.

Consider a Cooling-Off Period: In highly emotional conflicts, taking a break and allowing emotions to cool off can be beneficial. After a period of reflection, the parties involved may be more open to finding common ground.

Keep Channels of Communication Open: Even when initial conflict resolution efforts fail, it's important to keep channels of communication open. Sometimes, issues can evolve, or new information can lead to a resolution down the road.

Involve Higher Authorities: If the conflict is within an organization or community, it may be necessary to escalate the matter to higher authorities or management. They can provide guidance, enforce policies, or make decisions if lower-level resolution attempts have failed.

Review Policies and Procedures: In some cases, conflicts may be the result of underlying issues related to policies or procedures. It may be necessary to review and revise these guidelines to prevent similar conflicts in the future.

Document Everything: Organizations should keep a record of all communication, agreements, and actions related to the conflict. This documentation may be necessary if the conflict escalates to a legal dispute.

Team Building and Training: In workplace conflicts, consider investing in team-building activities or conflict resolution training for the involved parties. This can help improve communication and conflict management skills.

Agree to Disagree: Sometimes the only way to maintain relationships is to acknowledge that you have differing opinions or viewpoints, and you choose not to continue arguing. You don't have to see eye to eye on everything; you can choose to respect each other's right to hold different perspectives.

Acceptance: There may be situations where it's simply not possible to resolve the conflict, and acceptance is the only option. John Maxwell shares that there is disagreement, and then there is disrespect. In such a case, it's important to move forward, focusing on your own well-being by setting boundaries or disengaging from the situation or relationship.

Remember that every conflict is unique, and the approach to resolution should be tailored to the specific circumstances and individuals involved. Not all conflicts can be resolved to everyone's satisfaction; and in some cases, the best outcome might be a compromise or a mutually agreeable solution. Although we should always lead with a *Heart-Centered Approach* and have empathy, it does not mean you have to be an empath, take someone else's feelings on, and be the solution solver. An empath is like Velcro, and that can get heavy on our hearts. Sometimes, we need to be like wax paper and let that sh*t slide right off and *LET IT GO!* As we navigate ethical leadership in the next chapter, take what you learned about yourself here, and let your newfound self-awareness guide your commitment to forge a path of integrity and authenticity.

♡ HEART TAKEAWAY

Conflict... the worst that happens is that it leads to growth. We are human and conflict is inevitable! Don't allow your emotions to be hijacked, or be confused by passion. If you are unclear, be curious and ask questions! Remember: active listening is key; reflection is valuable; self-awareness is empowering; and engagement in open, honest, and empathetic communication is essential.

Heart-Centered ♡ Approach Story

When I work with clients, one of the most common conflicts in the workplace is between employees. Have you ever found someone too challenging at work, or encountered a colleague you disliked? A disagreement can escalate quickly when there are different personalities and working styles.

Imagine two employees, Sandy and Taylor, in a constant clash over differing working styles and communication preferences. Sandy, an extroverted, spontaneous individual, preferred impromptu discussions and brainstorming sessions; while Taylor, an introverted and detail-oriented colleague, valued structured planning and written communication.

The conflict reached a point where project deadlines were at risk, team morale was affected, and productivity declined. Recognizing the need for intervention, we facilitated a conflict resolution process. The initial step involved individual meetings with Sandy and Taylor to gain insight into their perspectives, preferences, and concerns. It became evident that their clash was not rooted in personal animosity, but rather in a lack of understanding and appreciation for each other's working styles.

The next phase involved a facilitated dialogue between Sandy and Taylor. During the conversation, both employees expressed their viewpoints, emphasizing the unique strengths they each brought to the team. We helped them identify common ground and encouraged them to explore ways to leverage their differences for the benefit of the team.

As a resolution, the team implemented a communication protocol that incorporated elements of both spontaneous collaboration and structured planning. Regular team-building activities and workshops on effective communication were also introduced to enhance interpersonal relationships within the team.

Over time, Sandy and Taylor developed a newfound appreciation for each other's strengths, and the conflict transformed into a catalyst for improved teamwork. The company witnessed enhanced creativity, improved project outcomes, and a more cohesive team dynamic.

This conflict resolution not only addressed the immediate interpersonal issues, but also contributed to a positive cultural shift within the team, fostering an environment where diverse working styles were embraced and used for collective success.

When managing conflict, using a neutral or third party can help resolve this issue to ensure everyone is working towards potential solutions while keeping in mind the common goal.

Ethics and Values

Guide decision-making, behaviors, and culture to inspire others and ensure the organization operates with integrity and a sense of purpose and fulfillment.

This will foster an environment built on trust, transparency, and accountability for employee morale and productivity and fortify the organization's reputation and its relationships with stakeholders.

Chapter 9

Navigating the Seas
of Ethical Leadership

The time is always right to do what is right.

—MARTIN LUTHER KING JR.

Ethical leaders act as a compass with the courage to stand up for what is right, even when it is challenging or risky. Leaders earn the trust of their teams and stakeholders when they consistently do what is right. A leader serves as a guide to ethical leadership when they demonstrate an unwavering commitment to set an example, exemplify the ethical behavior they expect from their teams and organizations, and inspire others through their actions and moral choices. As leaders, we face ethical dilemmas every day. As you navigate these seas, explore and ask yourself these thought-provoking ethical leadership questions in order to embrace authenticity and continuous self-improvement:

What example am I setting? Regularly assess whether your own behavior aligns with the ethical standards and values you expect from your team. This will ensure consistency between your words and actions.

How does my decision impact others? Reflect on the impact of choices to ensure that ethical considerations are prioritized, and decisions are made with the well-being of all stakeholders in mind.

Is this decision aligned with organizational values? This reflection will reinforce the importance of upholding the organization's core principles.

Am I listening to diverse perspectives? Consider a variety of viewpoints and experiences in order to make well-informed and equitable decisions.

Would my mom approve? I know you may be chuckling at this question, but would she?!

Let's explore the fundamental principles that sustain ethical leadership:

What is Ethical Leadership?

Ethical leadership is a moral and principled approach to guide and influence others within an organization. It encompasses the practice of making decisions and taking actions that align with a set of ethical values, principles, and standards. Significantly, ethical leadership places a strong emphasis on integrity, honesty, transparency, and accountability. It includes setting a positive example for others and consistently making choices that prioritize the greater good over personal gain. Ethical leadership fosters a culture of trust and responsibility and contributes to employee satisfaction, thereby reducing turnover and higher overall performance. This principled approach enables leaders to navigate complex ethical dilemmas.

The Importance of Ethical Leadership

Ethical leadership serves as the guiding light that helps steer the course of businesses and shapes the character of those who lead and follow. Ethical leadership is instrumental in enhancing a leader's character and credibility, maintaining a positive corporate culture, and building a strong reputation for an organization. In today's interconnected world, where information travels swiftly, an ethical misstep can tarnish an organization's image and erode public trust. Consistently making ethical decisions and upholding integrity will help fortify the organization's reputation, lead to increased customer loyalty, investor confidence, and brand equity, and foster a sense of purpose and fulfillment, all of which are critical for long-term success.

Ethical Decision-Making

Ethical decision-making is at the heart of ethical leadership. This process involves identifying the ethical dilemma. Leaders must recognize when they are facing a situation in which there is a conflict between different values, standards, or interests. Once the dilemma is identified, the next step is to gather information and assess the available options. This includes considering the potential consequences of each option on various stakeholders, such as employees, customers, and the organization as a whole.

Ethical leaders then need to evaluate the situation in light of their principles and values, using their moral compass to consider which decision is in alignment. In the process of resolving ethical dilemmas, it is essential to communicate the decision effectively, both to those directly affected and to the broader organization. Transparent communication helps build trust and understanding, even when individuals may not fully agree with the decision. Furthermore, ethical leaders must continually review and reflect on their decisions, remaining open to feedback and a willingness to adapt their approach as needed.

Ethical Leadership in Times of Crisis

In times of crisis, ethical leadership is a critical anchor that can help organizations weather turbulent storms. In challenging situations, such as natural disasters, economic downturns, or unforeseen crises like the COVID-19 pandemic, ethical leadership keeps the company steady and solid.

First and foremost, ethical leaders serve as beacons of consistency and reassurance to their teams. They communicate openly and honestly, ensuring that employees are well-informed about the impact of the crisis and the organization's response. Transparent communication builds trust, even when the news is unfavorable.

During crises, ethical leaders remain focused on their core values and the organization's mission. They guide their teams in upholding the organization's ethical standards, even in the face of adversity. Ethical leaders demonstrate the *Heart-Centered Approach* by recognizing the emotional toll that crises can take on their teams. They provide support, listen to concerns, and offer resources to help employees cope with stress and uncertainty. Ethical values are not situational but foundational to an organization's identity, ensuring that they emerge from the crisis with their ethical compass intact.

♡ HEART TAKEAWAY

Ethical Leadership's Summary of Dos and Don'ts

DO:

1. **Lead by Example:** Demonstrate ethical behavior in your actions and decisions, setting a strong example for your team and organization.
2. **Communicate Transparently:** Maintain open and honest communication with your employees and stakeholders.
3. **Show Empathy:** Demonstrate empathy and understanding when addressing ethical dilemmas and challenges.
4. **Promote Accountability:** Hold both yourself and your team accountable for ethical actions and decisions.
5. **Foster a Culture of Ethics:** Promote an organizational culture that values and prioritizes ethical conduct.
6. **Listen Actively:** Actively listen to employees' concerns, feedback, and ethical dilemmas.
7. **Provide Ethical Training:** Offer ongoing training and resources to help and educate all employees to make ethical decisions.

8. **Reward Ethical Behavior:** Recognize and reward employees who consistently exhibit ethical conduct.

9. **Promote Inclusivity:** Foster an inclusive environment where diverse perspectives are respected.

10. **Learn and Adapt:** Continuously educate yourself on ethical leadership best practices and be willing to adapt to changing ethical challenges.

DON'T:

1. **Compromise on Ethical Standards:** Never compromise ethical standards, even in challenging situations.

2. **Turn a Blind Eye:** Avoid ignoring or downplaying ethical concerns or violations within your organization.

3. **Conceal Information:** Do not hide or manipulate information to present a misleading picture of a situation.

4. **Tolerate Unethical Behavior:** Don't tolerate unethical behavior, even if it's exhibited by high-performing employees.

5. **Play Favorites:** Avoid showing favoritism or unequal treatment based on personal biases or relationships to different individuals or groups within your organization.

6. **Compromise on Core Values:** Never compromise your organization's values or principles for short-term gain.

7. **Neglect Employee Training:** Don't neglect to provide employees with the necessary training and resources for ethical decision-making.

8. **Neglect Ethical Feedback:** Don't ignore feedback from employees and stakeholders on ethical issues.

9. **Overlook Cultural Sensitivity:** Don't ignore the importance of understanding and respecting diverse cultural perspectives on ethics.

10. **Assume You Know It All:** Avoid assuming you have all the answers; be open to learning and growing in your understanding of ethical leadership.

Heart-Centered ♡ Approach Story

This ethical leadership story illustrates how when guided by the *Heart-Centered Approach*, values were prioritized over financial gain, which reinforced my commitment to ethical decision-making. My company faced an ethical dilemma in our recruitment efforts for a client. This client placed emphasis on only one factor: the diversity of each candidate.

While providing assurance about each candidates' qualifications and suitability for the role, the client persisted in questioning their diversity. The continuous emphasis on diversity over merit raised concerns about potential bias in the client's decision-making process. Recognizing the importance of upholding the *Heart-Centered Approach*, we decided to part ways amicably, as it became evident that the client's priorities did not align with our ethical principles.

Legal Considerations and Compliance

Uphold the rights of employees and protect the interests of your organization.

This will minimize legal liabilities and damaged reputations and maximize employee morale and workplace harmony.

Chapter 10

Stay OUT of Trouble
and IN Compliance

If you think compliance is expensive – try non-compliance.
—FORMER U.S. DEPUTY ATTORNEY GENERAL PAUL MCNULTY

Compliance is not merely a set of bureaucratic policies and procedures. It is the cornerstone of ethical and legal practices that uphold the rights of employees and protect the interests of organizations. Too often, clients call me after an issue has erupted. It takes more time and money to fix the issue than just doing the right thing in the first place. And, once the Department of Labor (DOL) comes knocking, I will need to introduce you to my Employment Law attorney friends – and their hourly rate is three times mine! Oh, and they have no bias on the size of your organization, so don't think because you have a small business, you will avoid a DOL claim.

My *Top 10 HR Mistakes Businesses Make* list will help you stay in compliance and out of trouble. Each of these mistakes, if left unaddressed – not *maybe* – but *will* result in significant costs. Not just in monetary terms, but also in damaged reputations, employee morale, and workplace harmony. Issues of non-compliance are like a volcano. They can take one day or hundreds of years to erupt. An active volcano has the potential to erupt continuously, so my recommendation is to be proactive versus reactive!

The Top 10 HR Mistakes Businesses Make

As we have discussed, employees are your number one asset. Depending on the size of your organization, whether it is the Business Owner, HR, Manager, or Supervisor, this leader is directly responsible for ensuring compliance with employment laws, fostering a positive work environment, and supporting the organization's goals. Again, I ask you to budget and invest in your leadership for proper training. Even experienced leaders can make mistakes because we are *human* and need regular reminders. Is the volcano ready to erupt in your organization? Because the steps below are just highlights of potential consequences, and important guidance on how to avoid them. However, reading about it is only the first step!

Ever since I had the opportunity to meet Lou Holtz, best known for being a football coach at Notre Dame, at the 2018 HR Florida Annual Conference, I have been passing his message along on three rules to live by. Keep these rules in mind as we address each mistake.

Lou Holtz's Three Rules

1. Do the right thing – make good choices.
2. Do everything to the best of your ability – don't look for excuses.
3. Show people you care – always.

1. Employee vs. Independent Contractor

One of the most common HR mistakes is misclassifying workers as either employees or independent contractors. This classification has significant legal and financial implications. Employees are entitled to benefits, such as overtime pay and workers' compensation, while independent contractors are not. Misclassifying can result in costly DOL or IRS legal penalties, back taxes, and damage to the organization's reputation.

To avoid this mistake, leaders should use clear and consistent criteria for classification. Ask yourself these questions:

Does this individual:

run their own business?

get paid upon completion of a project?

provide their own tools?

decide when they will show up?

what work they will do?

If you answered YES to any of these questions, this individual is an Independent Contractor. If you are ever in doubt, ask an expert to help you to determine the correct classification for each worker.

Examples of how you *will* get caught, not if, when you do not follow the Lou Holtz Rules:

- A worker files a complaint that they have been misclassified with the DOL... UH OH
- A worker has been classified as an Independent Contractor and files for unemployment... OOPS
- A worker has been classified as an Independent Contractor and was injured while working and tries to file a compensation claim... OH BOY...

A chart is available when you download the *Lead with Love* tools.

2. Classification: Exempt vs. Nonexempt

The misclassification of employees as exempt or nonexempt under the Fair Labor Standards Act (FLSA) is another critical error. Exempt employees are not entitled to overtime pay, while nonexempt employees are. Failure to properly classify employees can result in expensive wage and hour disputes, back pay claims, and fines.

To avoid this mistake, leaders must thoroughly understand FLSA and keep up with its evolving regulations. Regularly review job descriptions and ensure they accurately reflect the duties and responsibilities of each role.

To avoid this mistake, leaders should ask these questions:
Is this employee entitled to overtime or not?
Could the employee be paid a salary or an hourly wage, or just a salary?
Can the employee earn any amount per job, or must they earn at least $684 per week?*
Can the employee work in any field, or do they need to fit into one of the seven exemptions (Executive, Administrative, Professional, Outside Sales, Computer, Creative, Highly Compensated)?
Does the employee need to meet the Fair Labor Standards Act (FLSA) Duties Test to qualify for the exemption?

*Salary thresholds for FLSA may change. This is current as of this writing.

Depending on how you answered each of these questions will depend on the classification of your employee.

An example if you choose not to follow the Lou Holtz Rules – Facts: Your employee is Nonexempt. The organization has been paying them a $60,000 salary, and consistently works five hours of overtime (any hours above 40) each week. The employee has been employed for one year and quits because of a harassment claim and retaliation. (Note: A nonexempt employee can be paid a salary; however, this does not mean they are exempt from being paid overtime.)

- Employee is misclassified as Exempt... OOPS
- The organization does not show this employee empathy and care... TOO LATE
- Employee reports organization to DOL... GET YOUR CHECKBOOK OUT

- DOL comes knocking and now doesn't just look at this one employee... but looks at *all* 50!
- $60,000 salary is $28.85/hour with overtime pay at 1.5 times = $43.28
- Back overtime for the year: $3,751.80... but wait, there is more...
- Because unpaid overtime amounts are doubled as a penalty: $7,503.60... but wait, there is more...
- Add attorney's fee (yours and your employees) + MORE penalties + fines + back taxes on the unpaid overtime.
- This $7,503.60 just went to possibly $60,000 or more

This is no joke; your organization is not a playground, and the government does *NOT* play. Be a Lou Holtz and call an expert if you are ever in doubt!

A diagram is available when you download the *Lead with Love* tools created by Adam Hersh, Esq.

3. Bad Hires

Making poor hiring decisions is a costly mistake in terms of both time and resources. A bad hire negatively impacts five crucial areas: productivity, morale, performance, retention, and culture. Five characteristics to look for in a bad hire are poor quality of work, bad attitude, lack of skill set, consistently late, and not being a team player. Additionally, the cost of recruiting, onboarding, and training new employees can be substantial.

To mitigate this mistake, organizations should establish a robust hiring process (see Chapter 5). As a review, the five steps to avoid a bad hire are to ask good and compliant interview questions, check resume details carefully, be honest about the company and the team, focus on soft skills, and set up for success with a structured onboarding process.

A list of interview questions are available when you download the *Lead with Love* tools.

4. Onboarding and Offer Letters

Neglecting a well-structured onboarding process is a common HR mistake, which we discussed in Chapter 5. Two things to remember that are worth repeating: 1. Onboarding starts before the Offer Letter – it starts with recruitment; and 2. Create excitement and make it an experience! A successful onboarding program sets the tone for an employee's experience within the organization.

Karen's 7 Steps to Onboarding Success:

1. Recruitment
2. Office Visit
3. Offer Letter
4. Early Onboarding
5. Day 1 Welcome
6. Orientation
7. Ongoing Engagement

TIP: Create an Onboarding Checklist!

A sample Onboarding Checklist is available when you download the *Lead with Love* tools.

Inadequate onboarding can lead to decreased engagement, confusion, and increased turnover rates. Additionally, poorly drafted offer letters can lead to misunderstandings and legal issues. To avoid these mistakes, call an expert!

A sample Offer Letter is available when you download the *Lead with Love* tools.

5. Background Checks

Failing to conduct thorough background checks can lead to negligent hiring lawsuits, workplace safety concerns, and damage to the company's reputation. As we discussed in Chapter 5, remember not all arrests lead to a conviction. Don't assume the worst, and talk to the candidate. Second-chance employees sometimes could be your best!

David Miklas, Esq. also finds the best HR crazy stories. One story he shared with me for my *Top 10 Mistakes Businesses Make* presentation regarding background checks was how a cable company was ordered to pay $7 billion (not a typo) to the family of a Texas woman who was murdered by a repairman. The repairman lied about his past jobs and the cable company did not verify his employment. Had the cable company done their due diligence and conducted a background check, the repairman would have never been hired.

Please... do not... miss... this...step... and do your due diligence. Protect your organizations, your employees, and your clients.

6. Recordkeeping Requirements and I-9s

Inadequate recordkeeping and I-9 compliance can lead to severe legal consequences. The Immigration Reform and Control Act (IRCA) requires employers to verify the identity and work authorization of their employees by completing and maintaining Form I-9. If your organization has over 25 employees, you must E-Verify. If you look at your employee files right now, do you have the necessary records of who worked, when, and for how long? Would you pass an audit? These records protect the organization and the employee. If a dispute arises, you have the information to prove you are being a Lou Holtz! For each employee, organizations must track the following:

Full name and SSN	Time/Day workweek begins
Full Address	Basis on which wages are paid
Date of Birth	Regular hourly pay rate
Sex and Occupation	Total daily or weekly straight-time earnings
Total overtime earnings for the workweek, if applicable	Additions/Deductions from wages
Total Wages paid each pay period	Date of payment and pay period covered
Hours worked each day + in/out for lunch (nonexempt employees)	Total hours worked each workweek

In addition, it is important to have three separate files:

General Employment File	I-9 Records
• Employment Application • Performance Reviews • Disciplinary Forms • Basic employment information	Depending on the size of your organization, a binder with active employees and termed employees with A-Z Dividers. If you are a paperless office, keep a separate folder.
Medical Records File	
• FMLA* documents, if applicable • Disability-related documents • Protected confidential medical-related information in the event employment file is requested in a court matter	

*Family and Medical Leave Act

Records must be kept at the place of employment or in a central records office; length of time depends on the type of document and state and local regulations.

To avoid this mistake, call an expert!

7. Employee Handbooks

Not having a comprehensive and up-to-date employment handbook is a significant HR mistake. The Employee Handbook serves as a critical reference for employees, outlining company policies, expectations, and procedures. I am not sure which scenario is worse, a poorly crafted handbook that can lead to misunderstandings, disputes, and legal liabilities, or not having one at all. It is definitely a toss-up!

How many employees do you think you need to have an Employee Handbook? One is the correct answer! It only takes one employee for the volcano to erupt! If you have an Employee Handbook, when was the last time you reviewed it? Think of your Employee Handbook as an opportunity for a one-stop shop for information and protection. The Employee Handbook:

- Introduces employees to your culture, mission, and values.
- Communicates to employees what is expected of them, and promotes open communication and transparency.
- Educates employees on management best practices, logistics, and various entitlements.
- Clearly communicates key company policies, which management consistently refers to and communicates.
- Showcases the benefits your organization offers.
- Ensures compliance with federal and state laws.
- Protects you against employee claims.
- Provides employees direction to obtain workplace-related help.

Organizations should ensure that employee handbooks are regularly reviewed and updated to reflect current laws and organizational policies. In doubt? Have Questions? To avoid this mistake, call an expert!

8. Controlled Groups and Common Ownership Requirements

Many organizations overlook the implications of controlled groups and common ownership requirements. These rules can have a significant impact on employee benefits, retirement plans, and tax obligations. Here are some points to keep in mind:

- The controlled group rules are governed by the Internal Revenue Code (IRC) and the Employee Retirement Income Security Act of 1974 (ERISA).
- A controlled group exists when two or more entities are connected through common ownership.
- Any type of business entity can be a member of a controlled group for benefit plan purposes (corporation, partnership, sole proprietorship, or LLC).
- Common Ownership affects Affordable Care Act (ACA) Compliance Requirements of 50 or more full-time equivalent employees that are part of a controlled group and subject to "pay or play" penalties.
- Controlled group rules exist so that employers cannot use multiple corporations to escape coverage or nondiscrimination rules.

To avoid this mistake, call an expert *AND* follow the Lou Holtz Rules! Stay IN compliance with relevant laws and OUT of trouble.

9. Termination, Documentation, and At-Will Employment

Inadequate documentation and misunderstanding of at-will employment can result in wrongful termination lawsuits and legal complications. It's essential for organizations to document employee performance issues and terminations effectively, ensuring that they comply with federal and state laws. I will say this again in case you did not catch it the first time... DOCUMENT, DOCUMENT, DOCUMENT! Organizations will lose in any litigation if they have not thoroughly documented! Proof is always in the pudding!

When terminating, keep three things in mind: 1. Be *brief*; 2. Be *factual*; and 3. Be *compliant*! No matter how terrible that employee may have been, remember they are human. Just because you may live in an *at-will* state, think twice before terminating without cause or without warning, *especially* if you have not been documenting. Without documentation you may not avoid repercussions such as litigation for wrongful dismissal, and payment of damages!

Another critical reminder for organizations is to provide proper training to supervisors and managers on termination procedures and documentation. Organizations get in the most trouble when their supervisors and managers *say* or *do* something incorrect because they did not know correct procedures. The consequences of not training? *Big* money, so get your checkbook out. To avoid this mistake, reach out to HR or call an expert! Can't say it enough!

10. Leading with Compassion, Empathy, and Heart

The final mistake may seem counterintuitive. However, I know you are not surprised that this is on my list, as it is the subject of this entire book. We can all agree that no one is alone in their increased reliance on technology and data to do a job. One thing that no one has figured out, though, is how to automate empathy and critical thinking – two cornerstones of a successful leader. So, while learning to leverage new tools is important, we should never forget what the "H" in HR stands for – HUMAN.

H – Hearts

U – Unite

M – Making

A – Aspirations

N – Nourish

Being HUMAN is a collective effort. When hearts unite and come together with shared intentions and goals, individuals combine their passions, that creates a nurturing environment and fosters growth, fulfillment, and well-being!

The biggest mistake is leaders not taking the time to understand their employees and, instead, treating them like numbers on a spreadsheet. Please do not miss the fact your employees are human and have hearts. Do you have a pulse on them? Have the coffee talk – get to know them – be present. I give you permission!

To avoid this mistake, prioritize your number one asset – your people!

Heart-Centered 💛 Approach Story

Team Work Makes the Dream Work. I am an Ohio girl wearing Florida flip flops. My heart is faithful to my Cleveland teams, especially Browns football and Ohio college football, University of Toledo Rockets, and our Top 10 Ohio State University.

However, one of the best team speeches I have heard came from legendary Michigan football coach Bo Schembechler in 1983. Here is how he addressed the Wolverines:

*We want the Big Ten championship and we're gonna win it as a Team. They can throw out all those great backs, and great quarterbacks, and great defensive players, throughout the country and in this conference, but there's gonna be one Team that's gonna play solely as a Team. No man is more important than The Team. **No coach is more important than The Team. The Team, The Team, The Team, and if we think that way, all of us, everything that you do, you take into consideration what effect it has on my Team.** Because you can go into professional football, you can go anywhere you want to play after you leave here. You will never play for a Team again. You'll play for a contract. You'll play for this. You'll play for that. You'll play for everything except the team, and think what a great thing it is to be a part of something that is, The Team. We're gonna win it. We're gonna win the championship again because we're gonna play as a team, better than anybody else in this conference, we're gonna play together as a team. **We're gonna believe in each other, we're not gonna criticize each other, we're not gonna talk about each other, we're gonna encourage each other.** And when we play as a team, when the old season is over, you and I know, it's gonna be Michigan again, Michigan.*

Your number one asset is your people, surpassing any single leader in importance. Are you ready to take action?

Conclusion

A Call to Action

Now, it is up to you. You are standing at the crossroads of information and insight, and it is time to take action. You now have the knowledge; but this book is much more than that – it's an invitation to dance into transformation. Because in the rhythm of the *Heart-Centered Approach* is an opportunity to change the dance of leadership.

Reflect on your leadership journey. What do you envision after exploring the heartful journey of a wellness wonderland, navigating the seas of ethical leadership, and engaging in the adventure of conflict resolution? What emerges as your top three takeaways? Use this moment to identify these.

When will you start? What can you do tomorrow to herald a swift transformation? What can you do next week to orchestrate a deliberate shift? What can you plan to do next month? Setting your sights on a broader horizon of next year, what do you envision as a profound evolution?

This *Call to Action* extends beyond the written word; it is a roadmap for your ongoing leadership journey. As you articulate your responses, visualize the ripple effect of how your choices and your decisions will resonate within your team and organization. Allow your path to be guided by the *Heart-Centered Approach*, where leadership is not just a role but a profound human connection.

As you stand at the crossroads of assimilating these 10 **Principles of the *Heart-Centered Approach*** into your leadership methods and respond to the *Call to Action*, let these principles be the heartbeat of success pulsing through every leadership decision and organizational endeavor.

1. **The Heart-Centered Approach**
   Lead with compassion, empathy, and heart to optimize human potential.

2. **Leadership and Organizational Culture**
   Take action, influence change, and inspire others to create a sense of purpose and direction.

3. **Employee Well-being**
   Foster a workplace culture where individuals feel valued, supported, and empowered to navigate the demands of work and life.

4. **Employee Engagement**
   Nurture ongoing employee engagement efforts to boost positive outcomes for an organization's success.

5. **Recruitment and Onboarding**

    Attract top talent who possess the required expertise and soft skills, and who align with the organizational culture. Provide comprehensive orientation, training, and a welcoming environment.

6. **Retention and Turnover**

    Create a long-term commitment to value individuals for their unique contributions and holistic well-being.

7. **Change Management**

    Embrace change and be willing to evolve and adapt.

8. **Conflict Resolution**

    Accept that conflict is unavoidable, and understand it is our actions, reactions, and perspectives that make conflict an opportunity for critical conversation.

9. **Ethics and Values**

    Guide decision-making, behaviors, and culture to inspire others and ensure the organization operates with integrity and a sense of purpose and fulfillment.

10. **Legal Considerations and Compliance**

    Uphold the rights of employees and protect the interests of your organization.

Thank you for joining me on this quest to infuse heart and humanity into leadership. It is my hope that this book continues to serve as a guide, a source of inspiration, and a catalyst for change in the workplace with the *Heart-Centered Approach*. Always *Lead with Love.*

Enhance your *Lead with Love* journey using exclusive free tools!

Visit www.hrbykaren.com/leadwithlovetools to access and explore resources to elevate your leadership experience and thrive!

Acknowledgments

I extend heartfelt gratitude to those incredible individuals who consistently believed in my journey, challenging me to evolve as a leader, serving as a wellspring of inspiration, generously sharing their wisdom, and offering unwavering support from both near and far.

In loving memory of my parents, Laszlo and Arlene Leichtman, providing me with a foundation of faith, love, and the belief in me that I could accomplish anything I set my heart to. I miss them more than words could say, but I know they are looking down and smiling; and to all of my family whose love is unconditional, shaping my journey with warmth and strength.

In loving memory of my dear friend, Mindy Prizant. Mindy's enduring spirit illuminates my journey, inspiring me to live with purpose and meaning for both of us. This book is a testament to her profound influence on my life that continues to shape my path and purpose.

To my cherished friends, reflecting on our decades of friendship fills my heart with gratitude. Your enduring support has been a source of strength and joy, Stacey Elliot, Lisa Berliner,

Lisa Connelly, Steven Averbach, Stuart Braun, Sue Olman, Carol Van Nice, and my Virginia Beach Tribe...thank you for being the pillars of my life.

To my new community in Southwest Florida, your warm embrace has made me feel at home. In each interaction, I have found kindness, understanding, and a shared sense of belonging. Thank you for welcoming me with open arms, Kristina Overstreet, Kim LaMontagne, Randy Mitchelson, Scott Markowitz, Yaussy Casmartino, Yamirka Suyi, Michelle Borders, Barbara Saxton, Lindsay Burch-McLean, Alissa Desguin, Melissa Sweeney, Mark Fleagle, Natalie Poirier, Rich Williams, Jessica Hollomon, Cassie Schultz, Annie Meehan, Miranda Sharkey, Kristina Ribali, and all of my colleagues with the GROW Business Network, Naples Area Professional League of Executive Services, the SHRM HR Community, Naples Browns Backers, and the Chabad of Naples. I'm excited for the continued adventures and connections that await as we continue this journey together.

To my mentors, your investments in my growth have shaped not just my skills but also my character. I am grateful for the privilege of learning from you, Morton Bobowick, Esq. (deceased), Jo Ann Blair-Davis, JD, David Leichtman, Cindy Monroe, Nicole Tutko, Cecile Massé, Ph.D., Dani Lisong Wagner, Phil Gerbyshak, Michael Bean, Allison Blankenship, Andre Lehmann, Sergio De Cesare, Tim Hall, John Maxwell and Team, Kelly Merbler, Elisa D. Keller, Esq., Michelle Griffin, Damian Taylor, Esq., David Miklas, Esq., and Adam Hersh, Esq. Your influence will continue to be my guiding light, and I will carry your teachings with me on this journey today and always.

To my valued clients, your trust is the bedrock of our partnership. Thank you for allowing me to serve you. And to my dedicated assistant, Mackenzie Newhall, your hard work, happy heart, and support are the gears that keep everything running smoothly. Grateful for your commitment to our shared goals.

To April O'Leary, Publisher, and Heather Desrocher, Editor, and the O'Leary Publishing team for pushing me out of my comfort zone. Working with you has been an enriching journey and the collaboration is truly rewarding. I am grateful for the opportunity to bring my vision to life. Thank you for helping me make *Lead with Love* the best!

To my readers, thank you for being part of the journey with me and for taking these heart-centered strategies into your heart and business!

About the Author

Karen Shepherd, Owner of HR by Karen, LLC, Human Resources... from the Heart, was born and raised in Cleveland, Ohio. Before changing careers to Human Resources, she worked in the legal industry for 25 years, 21 years with the same attorney in estate planning and administration. In July 2020, Karen created HR by Karen, LLC to provide small to large business owners with tailored HR Solutions based on a company's strategic goals and objectives, helping businesses stay in compliance, saving money and administrative time, and coaching best practices for employee relations.

Her services include: customized HR consulting services, employee handbooks, professional recruitment, leadership training and facilitation, and being a high-energy, motivational speaker. As a speaker she presents on the topics of self-leadership, self-awareness, and the importance of a positive growth mindset. Karen regularly volunteers in southwest Florida, helping our future workforce with resume reviews and mock interviews, and providing free workshops for the business community on the *Top 10 Mistakes Small Businesses Make.*

In September 2022, the Naples Chamber recognized HR by Karen, LLC as Business of the Month. She has been quoted in several publications for her expertise in human resources, and voted *BEST* Human Resources company for 2023 at The Official Community Choice Awards - Naples.

Karen's professional background includes: a Master's Degree from Strayer University in Human Resource Management and Organizational Development, and proud recipient of the Outstanding Graduate Award; a Bachelor's Degree from the University of Toledo in Communications; Certified HR professional from the Society for Human Resource Management - Certified Professional (SHRM-CP); John C. Maxwell Certified Trainer, and DISC Certified.

To learn more about Karen Shepherd, her services, or to inquire about speaking availability, visit her website at:

www.hrbykaren.com

or follow Karen on Instagram, YouTube, LinkedIn, Facebook, and TikTok @hrbykaren.